# DENIAL OF A RESIDENCE PERMIT TO AN ELIGIBLE APPLICANT IN SWEDEN

FIRST EDITION

December 2022

# David Kayode Ogundedji &Johanna Granered- Ogundedji

Kindle Direct Publishing

Seattle, Washington, USA

First Edition of this book published in 2022

Editor: David Kayode Ogundedji & Johanna Granered-Ogundedji

ISBN: 9798365687226

Kindle Direct Publishing, Seattle, Washington, USA, 2022

# SUMMARY

When God created heaven and earth, and filled it with all necessary things, He had a vision. For God's vision to be fulfilled, He gave life to Adam and Eve. Both human beings made in the image of God were given the assignment to fill the entire earth in procreating descendants. They were also required to eat all fruits but not to touch the tree of life in the middle of the garden. Both Adam and Eve became disobedient to God and ate the fruit from the tree of life. Following disobedience to God, both of them were sentenced. Religious consider the sentence a curse. The price was worth paying. God's purpose was therefore prevented from being successful since the devil came into play. Finally, the earth was shared between the mindsets and behaviors of two different worlds. And this impacted either positively or negatively world societies through time and space. Over centuries and especially in this current century (XXIst) peoples are wicked human beings to the point that Human rights and fundamental freedoms are violated. Principles, rules, laws, norms and others that regulate institutions and civil societies are more or less existent. Accusation, disrespect, injustice, immorality, mistreatment, wickedness and all sorts of names become the day-to-day routine of various administrations at the global scale.

Some administrative systems are increasingly crucial in dealing wrongly with peoples while others protect human rights and fundamental freedoms worldwide. Both the purpose of God and international organizations such as the United Nations, Human Rights Watch and others whose ideologies consist of human beings to be treated equally with care, equity, impartiality, fairness and respect seem to be a failure. To render possible the abovementioned the Universal Declaration of Human Rights was proclaimed by the United Nations General Assembly in Paris on 10 December 1948.[1] Regardless of the importance of the declaration proclaimed on December 10, 1948, some European states give less attention to it and mistreat legal and eligible immigrants on their territories.

Consequently, the violation of universal declaration of human rights by states motivates advocates of social justice to intervene and expose entities practicing inhuman and degrading treatments against human beings in this current century. Actions taken by advocates of social justice are for the respect of human rights and fundamental freedoms. Peoples have to live on a peaceful planet today for a better future and perfect cooperation.

---

[1] United Nations, Peace, dignity and equality on a healthy planet, Universal Declaration of human Rights

Civilizations, people of diverse colors, organizations, institutions and others are inextricably bound together. Successful results are perceived when world populations proceed through fair cooperation. True cooperation policy is related to the respect of good- neighbourliness, the respect of Human Rights and fundamental freedoms.

No matter what laws are voted or ratified by international institutions or organizations, certain states by using special administrative titles alienate powerless, poor, inferior and socially deprived peoples and immigrants. Administrations such as the immigration service, the police and the debt collection became the generator of evildoers. Agents of these institutions react differently from the word of God and principles of fundamental freedoms that regulate the life of civilians. These three cooperate collectively with each other for making useless and unfair decisions for the most against immigrants. Following the inhuman attitudes legal or eligible immigrants are both denied temporary and permanent residence permit. From 2018 to 2022 a couple constituted of a Swedish married woman and mother saw her husband and father to her children kept in custody and deported from Sweden.

# TABLES OF CONTENTS

Summary…………………………………………………iii

Acknowledgment………………………………………...viii

List of abbreviations…………………………………ix

Introduction…………………………………………...1

Aim……………………………………………………4

Methodology and sources…………………………….9

Part 1…...……………………………………………..14

1 Background…………………...……………………14

Part 2……...…………………………………………..18

2 Theory......…………………………………………..20

Theory of justice…………………………………...21

Part 3...………………………………….....................27

3 Relationships…………………………...…………...27

Relationship with an African girl-friend ...……………28

Marriage with a Swedish lady…………………………30

Part 4...........................................................................33

4 Between custody and deportation........................33

In detention..................................................................34

Deportation..................................................................37

A come back to Sweden .........................................39

Analysis....................................................................43

Conclusion.................................................................73

Bibliography.................................................................85

# ACKNOWLEDGMENTS

I would like to seize this opportunity to be grateful to all those who contributed to the release of this book. Furthermore, I wish to express my appreciation and respect for all those who brought their contribution. My thanks go to each of you for visiting me when I was detained in custody at the Märsta detention facility. I would also like to thank you all who kept in touch with me when I was deported from Sweden to Benin; many thanks to Vendela Engström who wrote an article about the issue published on January 13, 2021 in the newspaper "*Arbetaren*". My greatest thanks go to my lovely wife Johanna Granered- Ogundedji who fought all the camp she could do to get me back to Sweden. I did truly she has been determined and bold enough to come down to Africa with my children and stayed with me over months. I wish to thank my dearest father-in-law, Sören Granered and my mother-in-law, Ann Gardeström who support me from near and far to the completion of this book. Last but not least, I would like to dedicate this work to my dear family (Family Ogundedji) which I have been separated from by force for three good years (2019-2022). By *David Kayode Ogundedji*

# LIST OF ABBREVIATIONS

**ECHR**      European Court of Human Rights

**LVU**        Lag om Vård av Unga (Child Care Act)

**OHCHR**    Office of the High Commissioner for Human
                    Rights

**UN**          United Nations

**UNICEF**    United Nations International Children's
                    Emergency

**UNCRC**    United Nations Convention on the Rights of
                    the Child

**UNTC**      United Nations Treaty Collection

**UtlL**        Utlänningslag (Immigration Act)

# INTRODUCTION

Immigration as a legitimate process moved populations for diverse reasons.[2] Some knew immigration for lack of economic opportunities, natural disasters and others for conflicts and political purposes or gender and religious issues. Immigration existed over centuries and centuries and today obligates world populations to leave initial positions for known or unknown destinations.[3] These movements are mostly motivated by the desire to discover other people and the search of employment opportunities or providing for safer places. This scourge affects millions of people of any age around the world.[4] The scourge of immigration during the last two decades of this century XXIst concerns populations of Third World states. Certain groups of Africans are therefore concerned with immigration activities. New Western countries are then discovered for the concerned ones.

---

[2] Robert Koulish, *Immigration and American democracy: Subverting the rule of law*, Routledge, New York & London, 2010, p.53-55

[3] Zvi Gitelman, *The new Jewish diaspora: Russian- speaking immigrants in the United States, Israel, and Germany*, Rutgers, The State University, New Jersey, 2016, p.45

[4] Terri Givens, Gary P. Freeman & David L. Leal, *Immigration policy and security: US, European, and Commonwealth perspectives*, Routledge, London & New York, 2008, p.4-6

Among these ones, David Kayode Ogundedji's case remains a typical example. As a native of Benin he emigrated to Europe and with final destination Sweden via Germany. After residing in Sweden within a period of months, David has obtained a temporary residence permit that allows him to work in the host country. He gets a work, pays taxes and started a new life in a private rental apartment. He regularly conforms his deeds to the Swedish immigration requirements. He has a perfect life and meets with a Swedish lady who he got married to in 2019. Later, David Ogundedji was faced with immigration issues when he still pays taxes. Regardless of the recurrent appeals introduced to the immigration services over months, David was kept into custody when his second born daughter, Gabriela Ogundedji, junior sister of Daniela Ogundedji born in 2017, came to life in 2020. On the way to the custody facility, David has been beaten and his face covered in blood (refer to medical report in the appendix). David's residence permit issue concerned Johanna Granered- Ogundedji, the mother of Daniela, Sandrine Lukula, his father-in-law, Sören Granered and Dr Ley Ikpo. All these people supported David Ogundedji for justice to be done on his behalf. The family business established by the Ogundedji in search of better living conditions for children and parents collapsed due to the fact that the immigration service kept David in detention facilities over months.

The family run up debts and was therefore reported for debt securities issued. Once released from custody after months, the applicant was deported from Sweden to Benin without any consentment. In view of this, his family was completely dispersed; Johanna Granered- Ogundedji remains with the legitimate children and Sandrine Lukula with the first born of the Ogundedji. Months later, Mrs Ogundedji travelled with the children, Gabriela and Isak to Benin where the family once again reunified. After spending months of vacancy with children in Benin, Johanna Granered- Ogundedji came back to Sweden in late September 2022. Following this, after suffering from injustice and mistreatment, David Kayode Ogundedji was given the opportunity to come back to Sweden and meet his wife and children, in November 2022. After being including in the Swedish system for years ago, David Kayode Ogundedji restarts from the very first beginning. He does so since the system wants him to restart from zero. As a committed father and good husband the applicant arms himself with courage in order to take good care of his family. For David Kayode Ogundedji family life is more important to him than being away. The head of the family is back to Sweden to guide and give needy children a better chance of a decent education.

# AIM

The book is written to shed light on how a residence permit application turned to the tragedy for the family Ogundedji. The narration is based on detailed and simplified information. David Ogundedji married to a Swedish lady, Johanna Granered- Ogundedji, in 2019 and also father of Daniela Ogundedji born in 2017, registered in the Swedish system with a personal number, was intentionally punished by the coalition immigration service- the police and the debt collection. Regardless of the taxes (between 6000 to 7000 Swedish crowns) the applicant paid for over seven years to the Swedish authorities since he has a permanent work, he suffers from injustice and mistreatment. Both physical and psychological forces were continually used on David Ogundedji from December 10, 2019 until April 29, 2021 before being sent to Benin.

During the period of injustice and mistreatment, the family Ogundedji in addition to his daughter Daniela Ogundedji and the mother of the little girl, Sandrine Lukula, all together endured the trauma caused by the abovementioned coalition. Both mothers (Johanna and Sandrine) and daughters (Daniela and Gabriela) including the applicant were subdued to human rights violation and fundamental freedoms.

The book is essential not only to shed light on the tragedy of the family Ogundedji unless it represents a signal for other peoples and families to be aware of the process of residence permit conducted by the Swedish immigration service. Regardless of the due procedure that this administration is said to implement and referred to residence permit applicants, there is another face of the false abundance coin that is not reveal.

We would like here to send strong signals from the tragedies of the family Ogundedji in order to make a distress call for applicants in the same situation as David Ogundedji. Through this story, we want to denounce injustice and mistreatment and bring our contribution to the eligible victims of the immigration service authorities. Our contribution consists in stopping the violation of Human Rights and social life. Violation of this type is considered a disaster unfolds tragically destroying lives and livelihood, families and economies.

We want therefore to deliver messages and to encourage applicants and families facing with similar tragedies not to lose hope and come out to fight a battle for legal battle for justice. We wish as coined by the philosophers, scholars, theorists, activists and others to let this disastrous system of coalition to be known at the international scale.

Once the issue would be spread worldwide this may contribute to the reduction of the number of victims. Being aware of the irregularities administered to applicants by the immigration services, justice shall prevail over evil. Ethics and morals will be promoted more actively worldwide through administrations and societies. To reach that level requires sacrifice and attention. The narration is a tiered checking, aiming at quickly motivating the weak and the poor applicants to get close to each other for forming bodies of stable and strong circle of voiceless. The associations of victim applicants will help affected peoples to recover psychologically and physically from injustice and mistreatment. Dissatisfied applicants need to react against abuses of power. Cooperation will unveil tragedies in order to be known so victims can be given assistance. Experts may help solving issues related to immigration rights. Challenges will therefore be solved and applicants shall not remain ignorant of the principles and laws concerning immigration and residence permit. Knowledge about rights and duties will be affordable to applicants for processes and procedures related to applications and issuance of a residence permit. The truth needs to be told and credit given each time injustice, condemnation, abuses, reprimand or alienation is unfairly applied to eligible applicants.

Lastly, the family Ogundedji needs therefore to be fully compensated for the injustice and arbitrary detention the father and husband suffered for years. Individual or collective manifestations have to be arranged for the Swedish government to know the side of the story from dissatisfied applicants, in cases where it has not a thorough knowledge of the situation.

The book is first written on behalf of David Ogundedji and his family members as well as victims, dispersed and destroyed families, academicians, experts or not. The redaction also concerns those keen to see the current investigations since the case was reported to the police station, on December 13, 2022, in order to have a better understanding of the impact of the truth whether academic, vocational or not. The writing consists initially in motivating the relevant Swedish authorities, international public opinion, international organizations, and international non governmental organizations to take action where necessary and act more effectively to protect the rights of the dissatisfied and afflicted applicants for Swedish residence permit in Sweden. The idea behind this is to create an appropriate environment for processing cases with fair trail, justice and respect for international human right law at the Swedish local level.

Once, attitudes of immigration, police and debt collection service authorities are considered crimes since they go against the principles of human rights as mentioned by the Universal Declaration of Human rights, these acts have to be condemned in a strict way.

Justice needs therefore to overcome injustice. For justice to take ahead of time in terms of injustice, strong controls have to be maintained in these administrations where alienation becomes the sole methods for immigration service, the police and the debt collection officers. The book aims to denounce the tragedy of the family Ogundedji caused by the coalition immigration service, police and debt collection so that shocks can be spread across the globe. The following is research question:

- Why did David Ogundedji suffer from injustice, mistreatment and deportation when he was eligible for a residence permit in Sweden?

Following the injustice, mistreatment and deportation experienced by David Ogundedji and family can it always be confirmed or not if eligible immigrants for residence permit are normally given the right residence permit in Sweden?

# METHODOLOGY AND SOURCES

The narrated story is a factual study which is scientifically documented. The tragedy of the Ogundedji concerns the suffering David Kayode Ogundedji experienced from 2019 to 2022 due to the immigration service. Collective injustice and mistreatment negatively impacted the Ogundedji. For the story to be considered credible, Johanna Granered-Ogundedji, one of the main living witnesses narrates with accuracy the empirical facts. The narration is detailed based on what happened. The narrator does not take any position despite of the fact that she is the wife of the victim. Credible narrations require authenticity since the story needs to be accepted in both the academic and scientific fields. A science- based approach is therefore important in the redaction of the book. Opinions and reports are confirmed and corroborated.[5] The methodology responds to scientific criteria.[6] Collected data in form of medical and administrative documents confirm the situations.[7]

---

[5] Ben Akpan & Teresa J. Kennedy, *Science education in theory and practice: An introductory guide to learning theory*, Springer, Cham, 2000, p.64-65

[6] Kofi Kissi Dompere, *The theory of knowledge square: The fuzzy rational foundations of the knowledge-production systems*, Springer, New York, 2012, p.158-160

[7] Sigmund Gronmo, *Social research methods: Qualitative, quantitative and mixed methods approaches*, SAGE, London, Singapore & New Delhi 2019, p.271-273

The book design is supported by evidence which makes of the story especially forensic accountancy. The credibility of information will lead readers to have a detailed and in-depth understanding of the contents of the tragic situation. The story is a family-based qualitative research. The qualitative method is mostly used for the completion of the book. At times, calculations comment on digits when necessary.[8] The narration is described with more qualitative precisions than quantitative ones. Sources are forms of newspapers, academic books, texts, laws, orders and testimonies. For the book to be accepted in the academic and scientific world, some terminologies are used. The terminologies are described to ease the understanding of context for those who are not familiar with them.

A terminology is a special assumption which scientists make use of in certain appropriate domains.[9] In view of this, words such as hypothesis, theory, observation, confirmation, rejection, analysis and conclusion are defined and associated with the writing of the book. The utility of the deductive reasoning here consists in measuring the level of the book in the scientific domain.

---

[8] Bruce A. Thyer, *The handbook of social work research methods*, Sage Publications, Inc., London, 2001, p.276-278

[9] Jeremy M. Smallwood, *The ESD control program handbook*, Wiley & Sons Ltd, New Jersey, 2020, p.1-2

The process fulfills the requirements of a form of design which starting point goes from a hypothesis and ends with a conclusion. From the starting point to the conclusion different stages are completed. The design responds to specific requests, usually from theory, observation, confirmation or rejection to analysis. A hypothesis regularly describes a phenomenon occurring in the natural world.[10] A theory represents carefully thought-out explanations concerning real life events.[11] An observation is related to the knowing and collecting or recording data.[12] A confirmation is the logical study of scientific hypotheses that are either confirmed or rejected by evidence.[13] An analysis is the second last place of the research. Each analysis gives a clear interpretation of the results after the conducted scientific experiment is completed and the problem is presented in a clear way.[14]

[10] James A. Marcum, *An introductory philosophy of medicine: Humanizing modern medicine*, Springer, New Jersey, 2008, p.243-245
[11] Jeanne H. Ballantine & Joan Z. Spade, *Schools and societies, A sociological approach to education*, SAGE, California & London, 2015, p.9-11
[12] Jean NcNiff & Jack Whitehead, *All you need to know about action research*, SAGE, London, 2006, p.137-139
[13] Gregory Feist & Michael Gorman, *Handbook of the psychology of science*, Springer, Publishing Company, New York, 2013, p.444-446
[14] Sven Ove Hansson & Gertrude Hirsh Hadorn, *The argument turn in policy analysis: Reasoning about uncertainty*, Springer, Cham, 2016, p.345-348

A conclusion is the last stage of an experiment. The conclusion links the measurements and observations and takes into account the summary of the results of a conducted and completed research.[15] Sources are of types of primary and secondary ones. The narrator, Johanna Granered-Ogundedji is an eyewitness. The Ogundedji family members and relatives as well as friends of David are all considered primary sources. Secondary sources interpret data used in the description of facts and is confirmed forensic and scientific.[16] Sources are in French, English and Swedish languages. Both the third person singular and the first person plural are used as the impersonal form in the story. The name Johanna is also mentioned regularly. The written language is English. English language is chosen for the book to reach many readers worldwide. The book is easy to read and understand the tragedy. The completion of the book fulfills the design of academic field since the facts are reliable, logical than emotional regardless of the sensitive side of the tragedy experienced by the family Ogundedji and relatives as well as others. The theory of justice is explains in chapter two for emphasizing injustice and mistreatment.

---

[15] Craig A. Williams & David V. James, *Science for exercise and sport*, Routledge, London & New York, 2001, p.152-154

[16] Richard K. Gardiner, *Treaty interpretation*, Oxford University Press, Oxford, 2015, p.462

The limit of the book is related to the title. The book demonstrates specific characteristics of the scientific approach. Page intentionally left blank.

# PART

# 1

# BACKGROUND

David Kayode Ogundedji is a native of Benin. He is a former police officer in his country of origin. For some special reasons, David decided to stop exercising as a police officer and leave Benin for another destination. His chosen destination is Europe but the choice of landing spot remains difficult since he did not have any idea about where to go. In view of differences existing in the conditions of choice, he was given advice from a friend living in Germany. This opportunity led him to come to Europe in 2013. The first country to be visited is Germany. From Germany he came to Sweden. Once in Sweden, David did his level best to comply with the immigration requirements. He met a Swedish lady and later they became a couple. Being living in Sweden for months, David was falsely accused of dealing with drug by an African. The accusation resulted in a fight. The police intervened in the issue and David was arrested and kept in custody. The arrestation has nothing to do with the accusation unless with David illegal situation.

The case of drug accusation was prosecuted and David was released after a two weeks period since he is found no guilty. He was compensated for the amount of 35 000 Swedish crowns. Despite of the fact that he was given compensation, the acquitted person was once again kept in custody at the immigration deportation camp. The weird thing is, David before being kept in custody his relationship with the Swedish lady ended. This time, David stays in custody for a six months period. Once released, he went to collect his belongings remained at his former companion's apartment. The day David came to her place and she saw him, she started crying and begged him to give her another chance for the relation to be saved for the future. After a long period of discussion and negotiation they forgive one another and the relationship have restarted. After a number of months, both David and his girl-friend travelled to Benin in 2014. Once in Africa, the partners got married and spent some days of rest in a lovely place. After the marriage ceremony and having spent good days together, the married woman flew back to Sweden. Eleven months later, David was issued a residence permit of a two years period. He came back to Sweden in 2015 as a legal resident in Europe, for the first time. Having had the residence permit allows him to work in Sweden. David starts working and paying taxes between 6000 to 7000 Swedish crowns monthly.

Unfortunately, before the two year prescription delay of residence permit, David's wife met another person and once again the relation ended. The relation was destroyed since the new boy friend-friend of the wife was a drug addict. The new partner consumed drugs in front of the children-in-law which David deems to be against since it is incompatible with the law (LVU lagen). The issue was reported to the immigration service and David was therefore rejected from the apartment. Over months, David met a new girl-friend but this time his companion is from Africa. The lady is a Congolese native. Some months later, David's new girl-friend got pregnant and later gave birth to a baby girl, named Daniela Ogundedji, in 2017. Before the birth of Daniela, David was confronted to his family-in-law which was against his relationship with Sandrine Lukula. This is another issue David has to deal with in addition to the problem opposing him to his former wife. Following the interruption of his relationship with the woman through whom he came to Sweden, the immigration service urged him to leave the territory. Regardless of the decision of leaving the country, David informed the immigration service to be into a new relationship and his partner is pregnant. The information was rejected by the immigration service and telling him that pregnancy is no guarantee for being issued residence permit.

According to the immigration service, the lady with pregnancy is not the person who allowed him to be granted a residence permit. Otherwise, in view of the issue that opposed David to the parents of his pregnant girl-friend, he decided to be into a healthier relationship. Following this constraint, he met Johanna Granered in 2018 to whom he got married in 2019. Before marriage, he explains all the truth concerning his situation to his woman to be, Johanna Granered- Ogundedji. However, aware of some of the details that have subsequently come to light, Johanna Granered Ogundedji got into contact with the immigration service. The contact with the immigration service was to help find solutions related to her partner (husband) residence permit issue. After contacting the case officer in charge of her new husband application, David got called by his former wife's boy-friend. He threatens him with violent messages and even told him to be deported from Sweden to Africa and will never be issued any residence permit. Following these threats, Johanna Granered- Ogundedji kept on being into contact with the case officer at the immigration service. Months over, she decided with her husband and having the first born, Daniela Ogundedji with them to visit the immigration service in Sundbyberg in late 2019. The visit at the immigration service led to a meeting with the social services in Telefonplan, since false accusations were reported against Johanna.

The meeting with the social services was successfully performed. Things worked on behalf of Johanna and her husband. The mother of the daughter, Lukula Sandrine, gave her approval to Johanna to contact Daniela Ogundedji whenever she wants since the accusation concerned the little girl. Following the situation which the immigration service lost, the case officer decided to report the issue to the border police so that David could be deported from Sweden. David and Johanna Ogundedji not knowing that going to the police border facility in Kungsholmen could lead to the arrestation of her husband went to meet the police officer in charge of reported case. Once in the police border facility, on December 10, 2019, her husband was arrested and sent to custody. On the way to immigration detention camp facility (Märsta) David was beaten in the van. He was bloody. A medical examination conducted by a medical doctor recognized by the competent authority confirms all kinds of mistreatment David Ogundedji has been victim of. In the detention camp, David was also falsely accused of having drug in the room when being kept in custody. He asked the case to be prosecuted which he won since he was found no guilty. After spending an eleven months period in custody, David was released in 2020 for a short period and later deported from Sweden to Benin, in 2021.

It was not only in November 2022 that he came back to Sweden after his wife Johanna with children, Isak and Gabriela Ogundedji travelled to visit him in Benin. The visit to the husband and father last for three months. This book is therefore written for the entire world to be aware of the tragedy of the family Ogundedji. The book shed light on injustice and mistreatment David Kayo Ogundedji went through intentionally plotted by the coalition authorities, immigration- police and debt collection services.

# PART

# 2

# THEORY

For this book to be accepted in both the academic and scientific fields, it has to enclose practical and theoretical approaches. Scientific researches require theoretical approaches for the logical sense of the work to be confirmed.[17] The theoretical framework corresponds to a scientific demarche as required in both social and hard science. The use of theory in any scientific work helps making the project to be considered a scientific research.[18] Despite of the differing results both sciences are conducted scientifically. Regardless of the differences in methods, the principles remain similar.[19] The theory explains here is the theory of justice. The theory is chosen since injustice and mistreatment is applied to an applicant for residence permit in Sweden.

---

[17] Georges Guille-Escuret, *Structures sociales et systèmes naturels, l'assemblage scientifique est-il réalisable?* ISTE Editions, London, 2018, p.66
[18] Ibid
[19] Paul Tannery, *Recherches sur l'histoire de l'astronomie ancienne*, Cambridge University Press, Cambridge, 2015, p.28-29

The theory is defined in this section since it has to demonstrate the contrary of what is not included in the theory of justice. The section describes what generates the theory of justice in order to contradict inhuman actions applied onto a victim of injustice and mistreatment. For the narration to be accepted, confirmed and not rejected, empirical facts underlying structural discrimination are enumerated. They are not only mentioned unless they are vital pieces of physical evidence. Evidence in this narration is recovered in the injustice and mistreatment scene. To demonstrate that actions against human rights and fundamental freedoms occurred, empirical facts are cited and compared with the theoretical approach.

# THEORY OF JUSTICE

Justice as the first virtue of social institutions is related to the system of thought.[20] This virtue of social institutions derives from the political philosophy that tends to shed light on problems concerning the contemporary social world.[21]For the world to be as developed by God and requested by institutions, societies have to be in accordance with the Act.

---

[20] John Rawls, *A theory of justice, Original edition*, The Belknap Press of Harvard University Press, Cambridge, Massachusetts & London, 1921, p.3

[21] Ben Laurence, *Agents of change, Political philosophy in practice*, Harvard University Press, Cambridge, Massachusetts, 2021, p.1

The theory of justice helps to have a better understanding of injustices encounter in our political life.[22] In proceeding in such a way give boldness to human beings to denounce what is right or wrong and to bring solutions for a better future. Justice that is mentioned in theory may be studied and find out if this is practicable in the real world. To ratify an Act in theory is a thing and its implementation is another thing to consider. The theory therefore only describes in depth the best method of proceeding with the elements of justice. This theory emphasizes the role of social cooperation.[23] Justice can be perceived differently according to scholars or conceptions. Justice is considered to be normative when it concerns the philosophical theory.[24] In this view, people have to think about justice. For others, justice is a utopia. Meanwhile, justice in Buganda is referred to societal norms and not to an elaborate code of laws.[25] Otherwise, justice is related to fairness.[26]

---

[22] Ibid

[23] John Child, David Faulkner & Stephen Tallman, *Cooperative strategy: managing alliances and networks*, Oxford University Press, Oxford, 2019, p.70-75

[24] Paul Voice, *Rawls explained: from fairness to utopia*, Open Court, Chicago & La Salle (Illinois), 2011, p.7

[25] Helen Buss Mitchell, *Roots of wisdom, A tapestry of philosophical traditions*, Howard Community College, CENGAGE, Singapore, 2019, p.384

[26] John Rawls, *Justice as fairness: A restatement*, Harvard University Press, Cambridge Massachusetts & London, 2014, p.29

Issues of theory and practice lead to situations of philosophy and action. In view of this, valuable political actions demand a realistic sense in order to consider obstacles peoples are faced with. Opportunities have therefore to be given attention realistically. They need to be dispatched with fairness and not unequally since each human being has the right to inviolability related to justice and which cannot be overridden.[27] Justice is, in this regards, against the loss of freedom. Justice prioritizes the equity for the majority. In prioritizing the majority does not justify the discrimination of the minority. Justice is for everyone. Plato considered justice not to be a mere strength unless a harmonious strength.[28] For Plato justice is both an order and duty of the parts of the soul.[29] In the republic of Plato, justice is referred to the payment of debts or giving to each what is owed.[30] It is also related to do good to friends and harm to enemies. Justice is extended to a variety of conceptions that are for the best of human beings. Justice is not destructive since it promotes the respect of laws.

---

[27] Paul Behrens, *Diplomatic law in a new millennium*, Oxford University Press, Oxford, 2017, p.160-170

[28] Dr Bhandari, *Plato's concept of justice: An analysis, The Paideia project on-line*, Twentieth World Congress of Philosophy, Boston, Massachusetts, 10-15 August 1998

[29] Ibid

[30] Joshua Mitchell, *Plato's fable: On the mortal condition in shadowy times*, Princeton University Press, Princeton & Oxford, 2009, p.137-140

Both Plato and Aristotle agreed on the fact that justice consists in spreading goodness and to be obedient to laws. Despite of the idea of elitist, justice is for poor and marginalized.[31] Rights secured by justice are therefore neither subjects of political bargains nor the calculus of social interests.[32] For Rawls injustice is not tolerable but shall be tolerable when it concerns a case that helps to avoid a greater injustice. This explains the reason why truth and justice are uncompromising.[33]

Otherwise, justice for Thrasymachus is nothing other than the advantage of the stronger.[34] This signifies that justice is for the stronger person who rules and to whom people have to obey to.[35] Hence, Socrates opposes Thrasymachus definition of justice and emphasizes that justice contributes to better life. In the mean time both Thrasymachus and Socrates agree on the fact that justice is beneficial.[36]

---

[31] Michael Wilcockson, *A student's guide to as religious studies for the OCR specification*, Rhinegold Publishing Ltd, London, 2003, p.17

[32] Rawls (1921:4)

[33] Liat Levanon, *Evidence, respect and truth: Knowledge and justice in legal trials*, Hart Publishing Plc, New York Dublin, 2022, p.1-5

[34] Jill Frank, *Poetic justice: Rereading Plato's "Republic"*, University of Chicago Press, Chicago & London, 2018, p.55-65

[35] Dr M. Fogiel, *Republic, The by Plato*, Research and Education Association, New jersey, 1999, p.10-15

[36] Curtis N. Johnson, *Socrates and the immoralists*, Lexington Books, New York, 2005, p.130-135

Regardless of the fact that both Thrasymachus and Socrates agreed on that justice is beneficial they disagree on the beneficiaries. Later, he came to pass that Thrasymachus contradicts himself based on how he defined first justice as anything that profits the stronger and further claims that justice is the advantage of another.[37] At this level there is a paradox in the definition Thrasymachus gives to justice.[38]

In sum, social justice is as defined by John Rawls in the contemporary century is referred to equal economic, political and social rights and opportunities for everyone. Social justice therefore concerns three focal points such as equal rights, equal opportunities and equal treatment.[39] Social justice aims to create the legal framework based on the cooperation of human interactions that leads to the formation of institutions.[40] In this sense, any violation of the rules of justice is punishable.[41]

---

[37] UK Essays, Trusted by students since 2003, Essays, Philosophy, Key claims made by Thrasymachus in book I, published on February 8, 2020

[38] David Roochnik, *Thinking philosophically, An introduction to great debates*, Wiley Blackwell, West Sussex, 2016, p.25

[39] San Diego Foundation, *What is social justice?*, published on March 24, 2016 and updated on July 11, 2022

[40] Susan Benigni Cipolle, *Service-learning and social justice: Engaging students in social change*, Rowman & Littlefield Publishers, Inc, New York & Toronto, 2010, p.25-30

[41] Anthony F. Lang Jr, *Punishment, justice and international relations: Ethics and order after the Cold War*, Routledge, London & New York, 2009, p.10-15

Justice needs therefore to be applied to societies with equity and has to be respected by all with no distinction between individuals no matter what the gender, the race, the age and social classes. From antiquity to the contemporary period, theorists, philosophers, scientists and others fought and still fight for justice to achieve the purpose for which people debate and come up with adequate solutions for a good governance of civil societies. Regardless of these efforts, certain groups of people seem to still advantage the idea of Thrasymachus concerning his definition of justice.

# PART

# 3

# RELATIONSHIPS

A relationship is a connection of two or more people or characters.[42] There are various types of relationships.[43] In this context we describe the relationship of two people that are connected to one anther through love. In this precise case study this love is based on emotions. The type of relationship we are concerned with here is related to the one of David and his two last love stories with Sandrine Lukula and Johanna Granered. David did not enter a relationship with both of them at the same moment. No, he finishes one and enters a new one due to situations he was faced with. It has nothing to do with the choice of partner unless certain realities that motivated him to move from a situation to another one. David had a troubled relationship with Sandrine Lukula due to the reaction of the parents of this lady against David Ogundedji. David was therefore in the obligation to move one.

---

[42] Torion Kent, *Love yesterday, today and future tomorrows: Inspiration through notes, music and quotes*, 365 Love Publishing, USA, 2013, p.55-60

[43] Miriam Yvette Vega, *Relational schemas and condom-use in heterosexual relationships*, University of California, Berkeley, 1999, p.3-6

## *Relationship with an African girl-friend*

In 2014, after being separated from his first wife for drug issues David reported to the immigration service, he met Sandrine Lukula. One day in the city in front of Åhlens City, David met Sandrine. They started talking and changed phone numbers. Some days later, David took the first step and called Sandrine. The discussions were fruitful. Both of them came to an agreement to meet in the city. The meeting was perfect since they spent a lot of good time together. In the end they decided to regularly meet. Over months David and Sandrine became a couple and live a decent relationship. Few months later of happiness, Sandrine was pregnant. When the parents of the lady found out that the daughter is pregnant they started demonstrating opposition to the relationship of David and Sandrine. A thing to be clarified here is that David is from West Africa and his companion from Central Africa. In a word, Sandrine is a native of Congo while David is from Benin. Both of them are Africans. Regardless of the fact that David and Sandrine are Africans, the parents of the lady are not for the principle for both lovers to be coupled since David is not a native of Congo. The parents of Sandrine opposed the fact that David is not from Congo. As for them this is impossible that Sandrine will be coupled with someone from Benin. They emphasize and wish that the partner of their daughter has to come from the same country like them.

In the mean time David and Sandrine continue the relationship. Once in a time, Sandrine decided not to be into contact with her parents since she considers her progenitors to be a problem for her and her relationship. She was so in love David that she makes a decision not to meet then for a while. She did not fight with them unless she avoids meeting them since she was aware about the fact that they will always discuss the David issue and also about the pregnancy she bears. Since she has no contacts with relatives she was taken care of her boy-friend, David. For lowering the expenditures of David related to her she gets into contact with the social services that helped her with accommodation. Once she was offered a place to stay, the boy-friend, David bought the first necessity. David prepares the unborn's trousseau. Day in day out, the situation with Sandrine's parents became worse for David. Sandrine's parents accused David of things that he has no knowledge of. Since the parents continue to stress and harass David, the boy-friend decided to take care of his partner but will not continue being involved in the relationship. He therefore moves on and remains alone for a period of time. David concentrates on his work and other activities for a better future. He counted with the baby who he will be taking care of when it is born. He saves money for the baby to be and planned for the delivery. David considers himself a father even though the child was not yet born.

Still David has in mind that the parents of Sandrine will soon or later create him problems since because of him their daughter does no longer meet tem. In view of this, David who hàs to regulate his residence permit situation could not count with Sandrine to make it met Johanna Granered in 2018. Once he meets Johanna there was no chance for him to return to Sandrine since he was aware that he is not from Congo as Sandrine's parents assume. David gives a chance to himself to be with Johanna after a long period of celibate. He ended that period and started a new relationship with Johanna Granered who is a Swedish citizen.

### *Marriage with a Swedish lady*

Fortunately, when a door is closed another one is opened. David was then blessed for meeting Johanna. The story about Sandrine is closed. David met a new girl-friend named Johanna Granered. He picked her from her own world and brought her into his corporate scope. Johanna did no longer live as she used to do. She is attached to David and everything she does was related to the new boy-friend. Both start visiting regularly. David goes to work and comes back home some minutes later Johanna is around and both of them spend time together. Over months, Johanna introduced her new boy-friend to her parents. David is loved of Johanna's father, Sören Granered.

David noticed the difference between the parents of Johanna and the ones of Sandrine who caused issues to him. He was then confident with the relation he enters with Johanna. Once he trusted his new girl-friend, Johann, David opens himself to her and speaks all the truth about his residence permit application. Johanna hundred percent sure of spending the rest of her life with David, contacted the case officer of her new partner. She tries to better understand the situation. After being in contact with the case officer, David got called by the boy-friend of his former marriage who harassed him. To have contacted the case officer to settle the matter of residence permit led to new rivalries between the former wife and the new girl-friend of David since the one in charge of the application of Johanna's new boy-friend created a specific problem. David was said to be deported. Johanna and David did not go this way unless they tried to solve the issue. Johanna started getting into with lawyers to have her partner situation solved. She tried her level best to come up with better and efficient solutions. Johanna was hundred percent involved in this. When trying to have her partner to live legally in Sweden she at the same time finds ways to create conditions that will efficiently enable the eligibility her partner with no hindrances. Johanna makes a step and booked a time for their marriage to be celebrated. In August 2019, Johanna and David got marriage.

They had a great wedding ceremony where more than hundred persons were invited. The festivities were narrated by many in the city of Stockholm depending on the guests who took part in the party. The parents of Johanna were even present and honored that day. They were proud of their daughter and their in-law since he brought a change in her life. David was also happy since he considers himself loved by his in-law. The happiness that animated David was in comparison with Sandrine's parents who fought him regularly. David and Johanna were happy ones. The ceremony started and ended as they wished then. Following the ceremony Johanna Granered became Mrs Johanna Granered- Ogundedji. The coming days confirm the love of both Johanna and David through their attitudes. They were always together if they were not working. In the city the new married couple appears everywhere together. They were lucky to be together. On top of their joy, Johanna got pregnant. In this view, she keeps on fighting for the residence permit issue of her new husband and future father of the baby to be. Johanna took the issue of residence permit to different law firms. Having contacted various law firms, Johanna decided to personally discuss with the case officer in charge of the application of her husband in Sundbyberg in November 2019. Following this she went to the border police on December 10, 2019, Davis is arrested and kept in custody.

# PART

# 4

# BETWEEN CUSTODY & DEPORTATION

On December 10, 2019, Johanna and her husband went by their own to the border police office in Kungsholmen. The reason behind the motivation is that the couple wanted to come to any agreement with these authorities. The agreement concerned the applicant decision of residence permit. How to make things worked perfectly. In sum, they were ready for a compromise. Following this, the applicant life became a mess when his wife showed up at the immigration facility in Sundbyberg. From December 2019 to April 2021, David was kept in custody. On the way to the camp facility, the applicant was beaten by two police officers in the van. He was hurt and bloody. In order for him to have evidences related to his misadventure that occurred in the van, once arrived at the camp he contacted a medical doctor for check up.

## *In detention*

David visited the public health centre of the deportation camp at his arrival. He was issued a medical report which he requested from the medical doctor (refer to attachments in the appendix). His first day at the deportation camp was absolutely unsatisfactory in terms of psychological and physical health. David was mainly affected by the inhuman actions of police officers who harm him. The following days were not even peaceful no matter what the applicant did his level best to adapt himself to the deportation camp. He was recurrently enslaved since injustice and mistreatment were his daily tasks or companion. The mistreatment the applicant is victim of would be associated with the pandemic period. David was among people he did not know but was in the obligation to cooperate with since he was incarcerated against his will by the border police and the immigration officers. December 2019 was the moment the corona pandemic affected China and was later considered at the international scale, in March 2020.[44] From December 2019 and March 2020, David was kept in custody.

---

[44] Mark Zanin & Cheng Xiao, *The public health response to the Covid-19 outbreak in mainland China: A narrative review*, Journal of thoracic disease, Vol 12, No 8 (August 2020)

After being unlawfully beaten by police officers, the barrier measures were not respected in the deportation camp where the applicant was kept in custody. David was therefore contaminated of corona. He got sick for a long period before recovering. The applicant got weak and lost appetite. He was even not used to the food served in the deportation camp. Johanna, Sandrine, Johanna's father and others were therefore in the obligation to bring meal that David loves to the deportation camp. Months over months, Johanna travelled from Upplands Väsby and Liljeholmen even from diverse destinations to Märsta for supplying her husband with food. The suffering of her husband weighed heavily on her and her pregnancy. Not only Johanna was psychologically and physically exhausted unless her mother, her father, her sister and brother as well as the mother of Daniela, Sandrine Lukula well all concerned with the issue of detention of the applicant. Johanna was left with no chance to take care of herself and her pregnancy than travelling from various starting point to the deportation camp. David did not spend for the first time Christmas with his wife and child Daniela since he was kept in custody. David was not allowed because of the decision some immigration officers and border police agents came up with concerning the applicant.

Otherwise, his health estate once he gets contaminated by the virus of corona, David could no longer eat what comes from the refectory of the detention camp. The day Johanna was also sick and could not make it, David was left with no food. He sleeps empty belly and at times could not close eyes since his mind is filled up with tragedies. He is troubled and remained awake until the following day. At times David sleeps in the morning when other detainees start their day. After the situation of sickness and diet, the applicant was a victim of a plot. The plot consisted in accusing him of having drug on him. For the plan to be successful, a detainee was sent to the room of David with drug. When the detainee left the room, the detention agents proceeded to a control in the room. David was arrested since drug was found in his jacket. The plot failed and could not be used against David to be continually kept in custody and later deported since a witness the detainee who entered the room and put the drug in David's jacket. Following this, David requested the case to be prosecuted. Once the case was prosecuted, with the help of the witness, David won the case at the court. Regardless of the fact that the accused was not found guilty, he was not compensated. The weird thing with the accusation is that once the drug was put in David's jacket, the one fulfilling the action was released from custody the following day.

The rapid release of the detainee from custody confirms the accuracy of the plot. Despite of the won case, David was sent back to custody and with no compensation will be paid to him for the unlawful accusation he is accused of. In the following months David will be deported from Sweden to Africa. Months after a short release from custody and a few time spent with family, force was used on David and he was deported from Sweden to Benin.

## *Deportation*

In April 2021, David spent a certain period with his wife Johanna and children. One day he was about to show up to the border police when he got arrested once again. Later he was deported to Benin by the border police. When he went to the border police office it was just to present himself to them as he usually did and also has certain complaints about the immigration service. Unfortunately, David was caught in the trap of the border police and the immigration service. A flight ticket was already bought there was no choice for him than travelling to Benin against his will. David was escorted by two civil police officers. From the border police facility he was taken to the airport (Arlanda Airport). During the journey, they transited to Paris Charles-De-Gaulle (France) for Benin.

The deportation occurred since the French consulate in Benin issued a lasses-passer since the Beninese authorities refused to do so. The reason for which the Beninese authorities denied a lasses-passer to the applicant resides in the fact that David was married to a Swedish woman and has children registered in the Swedish system. Once at the international Airport of Benin, David was left to the Beninese border police officers by the two Swedish police officers. These ones returned to Sweden with the same plane the deportation occurred. David was questioned by the Beninese border police officers and after a period he enters the territory.

Somehow, a bribe has been paid by the French consulate in Benin for the applicant to enter the country he was supposed to be sent to. He was later told to apply for his residence permit from a Swedish embassy before coming to the host country. David lived difficult moment in Benin since he was left with no choice and no revenues. During his stay in Benin, the applicant was still into contact with his wife and children with whom he communicated through video calls. He regularly talked to them in the morning, in the day time, in the afternoon and in the evening before they sleep. They were then in constant contact. The relationship became then a distant one. Felling this difficult the woman tried by all means to be close to her husband with the kids.

At one point, Johanna planned and took with her the children to travel to Benin for visiting the husband and father, David Kayode Ogundedji. She did not only plan to travel but she also decided so that the dream can come true. She prepared herself. She bought the flight tickets that cost a lot from the remaining saving she has to live on with the children. Johanna Granered- Ogundedji made a sacrifice. In August 2022, Johanna Granered- Ogundedji with Gabriela and Izak Ogundedji travelled to Benin as planned.

### *A come back to Sweden*

After a stay of seven months of the applicant in Benin, Johanna Granered-Ogundedji could no longer take it anymore and travelled to Benin with the kids for visiting David Kayode Ogundedji. But before the visit, an application for residence permit on behalf of her husband was filed in advance. Once in Porto Novo, the family got unified and the only remaining one for the family to be completed is Daniela. She did not come with her mother-in-law, Johanna, since she lived with her mother, Sandrine Lukula. Otherwise, the journey went well and both Johanna and the children were happy to meet their father after a long period away from them. All members of the family Ogundedji were more than happy. Johanna Granered- Ogundedji, Izak and Gabriela Ogundedji stayed for a three months period in Benin.

The kids were pleased to be with their father since they have activities together. The family organized outing to be constantly and travelled around the Capital city of the country. The warmth and life in community gave a new start to the children who were no longer lost than they used to be in Sweden. They started gaining confidence in themselves. In the mean time, Johanna continued to contact the immigration office from Benin. She regularly called and also emailed them for her husband application to be given a response. The communication between Johanna and the immigration service was not easy but she did her level best to gather all the requested documents. All the documents were collected and sent to the case officer in charge of the application of David Kayode Ogundedji. Later, the applicant was given an appointment at the Swedish embassy in Abuja where he got interviewed about his relationship with Johanna Granered-Ogundedji. Once the interview was completed, Johanna did not give up unless she fought for the decision of her husband to be known. When she was sure that her husband would be issued a residence permit, she than took with her the children and travelled back to Sweden. Over weeks, the applicant was informed that he was issued a Swedish residence permit. Unfortunately, the type of residence permit that is issued is a temporary one.

The duration of the residence permit is for a two years period regardless of the eligibility of the applicant for a permanent residence permit. David was then given the opportunity to come back to Sweden for joining his family who visited him for months ago. The applicant waited then for the residence permit card to be issued before coming back to Sweden. In November 2022, after a long period outside Sweden, David came back to Stockholm and lives with his wife Johanna and the children Gabriela and Izak Ogundedji. He takes good care of the kids for whom he cooked the food, shower them and take them to the kinder garden. Johanna and the children seem to be happy since they once again unified. On week ends Daniela joins the family and played with her siblings to whom she shares love. The children are happy and they grow well and the father and the mother, all together are feeling well than before. The family Ogundedji is a beautiful family that wants to restart from the first beginning and make it as they planned for years ago. We do not know what will be next with the inhuman actions of the combined unit since David has only been issued a temporary residence permit. We hope that the immigration service will properly deal with the permanent application of David. We wish that this time will be the best since there has been a change in government. We hope that the political system is not the same; otherwise, we will consider the principles similar and the methods different.

Our wish is to promote justice through this narrated tragedy that is in a written form. The main purpose behind this is to share the suffering of the family Ogundedji with all human beings and to be dispatched all around the country and at the international scale for the truth concerning residence permit application to be known. In 2013, David came to Europe. He first lived in Germany before coming to Sweden where he met a lady and got married to her in Africa.

Once back to Sweden since he was issued a temporary residence permit, he worked and paid taxes. The first relation that brought him to Sweden collapsed and thenafter he met the mother of his first born daughter, Daniela. The situation David encounters with the parents of his second girl-friend motivated to look for a safe relationship. He then met Johanna to whom he got married to. The new wife was waiting for a baby when David was stressed by the combined unit to have him deported from Sweden. After years of resistance, David was deported from Sweden to Benin in April 2021when he was father to three children among whom Daniela (5 years old), Gabriela (1 year old) and Izak (some months). The family reunified since Johanna and David Ogundedji fought a peaceful fight for the husband to be issued residence permit. In November 2022, after being spent a long period of separation from his wife and children, David came back to Sweden.

# ANALYSIS

The work is to shed light on David Kayode's situation experienced during 2018 to 2022 when he was denied Swedish residence permit, arrested, kept in custody, deported and did a come back to Sweden in late 2022. David Kayode Ogundedji's life as a living testimony is released in a written form. The testimony by David is narrated by his wife, Johanna Granered- Ogundedji, mother of his children, Isak and Gabriella Ogundedji. The reason for sharing David's tragedy to world populations is for the story to be known at the international scale. It will not be fair for the inhuman situation to be kept only within the family Ogundedji. Injustice and mistreatment have to be denounced worldwide since they are forbidden. These actions are punishable by laws.

Regardless of his eligibility for the Swedish residence permit, David became a victim of the coalition immigration service-police and debt collection since he was unlawfully treated and deported. These combined authorities negatively impacted David's family life. They intentionally behave with disrespect, violation of human rights, torture and ill-treatment in order to harm the Ogundedji both physically and psychologically.

This book narrated by Johanna Granered- Ogundedji is released in order to lighten the load of physical and psychological burden and pain the family endures. There is therefore no choice than breaking the silence. The publication of the book tends to appease the suffering of victims of the Swedish immigration. Injustice currently leads to the mistreatment of victims when it comes to the issue related to residence permit. Justice is therefore required in the processing of cases of residence permit.

## *Theory of justice*

Justice as the first virtue of public life is as important as anything else. It is very important for human beings. Once it is vitally important, philosophers, theorists, scientists and advocates of social change and human rights emphasize that justice should be the central focus of preoccupations and decisions for civil societies. The notion of justice itself was therefore rooted in a shared belief that created debates between philosophers and scientists from Antiquity to today. If justice was not important it should have never engaged peoples in debates. The story of justice is central to world population history. It is through justice institutions and civilians can be regulated. Justice promotes awareness of the laws to ensure equity, equality, respect for human rights and fundamental freedoms.

Since justice constitutes the centre of debates through space and time this signifies that it is not easy to satisfy the fairness of the procedure. This difficulty, at times, creates imperfection. From this fairness imperfection certain people or authorities exercise injustice against the weak, the poor or foreigners. In this regards, the idea evoked by Thrasymachus in his definition of justice prevails. Once, human beings have it in this way; human rights are then violated regularly worldwide. For not allowing the propagation of injustice at the international scale some specialized agencies, judicial institutions, grass-roots and human right NGOs are promoted. The promotion of justice worldwide confirms that world populations are unfairly treated and their rights are therefore denied. Human rights abuses are nothing significant since they do neither promote economic growth nor human development. The only stupid thing it encourages is injustice. A state or a territory that currently favors injustice may actually not be considered democratic. Democracy promotes fair justice for all. Regularly European states are said to be democratic. An entity cannot be considered democratic and still implements injustice. In view of this, the territory cannot be continually said to be a democratic state. Either the state is democratic or undemocratic. To be given the status of democratic and sovereign state and act unlawfully against weak, poor and foreigners goes against human rights.

In the case a state is said to be democratic and denies justice to the alienated ones and keeps on violating human rights without interference, then justice is only in theory and not in practice. Otherwise, institutions are protecting each other. In this regards, there is no need for these judicial institutions to be promoted. What needs to be done is to redefine justice or reform the institutional systems of human rights. Once peoples for whom human rights is promoted are victims of injustice and nothing is done in this regard, then justice does not exist. If justice is non-existent this signifies that Thrasymachus definition for justice overtakes the one coined by John Rawls when we refer to the case of David Ogundedji in Sweden. Otherwise, justice has to be for all human beings since it is the first virtue of civil societies and institutions. Advocates of social justice have to step up their efforts to reduce injustice worldwide, otherwise their will and determination must be veil. For their efforts not to be nil, they have to continually fight and denounce injustice and promote justice for the entire world to be a peaceful territory as wanted by God and human rights activists. The Swedish immigration service as well as those combined into a single unit must be conformed to current legislation, regulations and ethical rules in the country. Sweden is not an anarchic entity unless a democratic state.

Swedish authorities need therefore to exercise primary through fairness and rules of social justice. The Swedish immigration service and accomplices may supposedly change work strategies since a new government is appointed during the month of September 2022. Regardless of the change in political system more attention needs to be paid to the new political alliance that governs nowadays. Former scholars, theorists, philosophers and human rights activists did their part; it nowadays depends on the good will of world populations and institutions to implement justice with fairness for a safer, healthier and peaceful planet. In sum, justice has to be shared by all and for all. Meanwhile, injustice is taking over from justice.

### *Injustice and mistreatment*

David as a native African in Sweden got married to a Swedish citizen, Johanna Granered in 2019. He was not only in a serious relationship through marriage unless a baby girl was born from the couple. The new born named Gabriella Ogundedji knew days in 2020. Previously, David was a father of a little girl, Daniela born in 2017. Various options allowed the applicant to hold a Swedish residence permit. Based on the abovementioned, the applicant was supposed to be given a residence permit since he meets the criteria of Article 2 kap.

5§ UtlL of the basic regulation.[45] The applicant meets all kinds of other criteria concerning issues related to insuring residence permit. What was then the reason for which the applicant was denied what is instituted by the Swedish law and government? Once voted, defended and promulgated, laws have to be respected and enforced regardless of the color, gender or identity of the person. People are all equal in front of the law since no one is above it.[46] Laws have to be implemented fairly and transparently.[47] In the case of David, the applicant suffers from injustice and mistreatment. The coalition migration service-the police and debt collection decided to harm the family Ogundedji. Residence permit was restricted to the applicant in 2019 even though he meets all criteria of eligibility. Having treated David in such a way emphasizes the confirmation of injustice and mistreatment against the applicant and his family. The perception of misuse of power can be related to the fact that the Ogundedji's went to the immigration service in October 2019 for the issue of residence permit to be solved.

---

[45] Uppehållstillstånd får beviljas efter inresan om utlänningen har stark anknyting till en person som är bosatt I Sverige och det inte skäligen kan krävas att utlänningen återvänder till ett annat land för att ge in ansökan där

[46] Andreas Frank, *Committed sensations, An initiation to homosexuality: The gay & lesbian*, handbook & compendium on coming-out & same- sex partnerships, Nordersted, 2020, p.255-260

[47] Eleni Kosta, Ronald Leenes & Irene Kamara, *Research handbook on EU data protection law*, Edward Elgar Publishing, Inc., Cheltenham & Massachusetts, 2022, p.250- 255

Once there, the immigration officers in charge of David's case could not justify the fallacious pretext (the decision). Applicants who meet all criteria of residence permit have to be treated alike with fairness, equality, respect and compassion once they submit applications. Cases must be processed fairly since justice is the first and highest virtue of both human beings and societies.[48] Based on the Universal Declaration of Human Rights, all human beings are equal in dignity and rights.[49] Once human beings are all equal, David's application should have never been treated differently. It needed to be similarly proceeded like the others in his situation. David did not need to be a victim of the immigration service which intentionally associated two other administrations to its methods used against the applicant. Injustice and mistreatment have been applied against the applicant over months and years. Separation with his family would have not been occasioned and rendered possible. David as father and husband has the right to reside in Sweden since he was eligible for residence permit. He was unlawfully detained in custody facilities for months.

---

[48] N. Sullivan & L. Mitchell D. Goodman, *Social work with groups: Social justice through personal, community, and societal change*, Routledge, New York & London, 2013, p.25

[49] United Nations, Universal Declaration of Human Rights, Preamble, Article 1, *All human beings are born free and equal in dignity and rights. They are endowed with reason and conscience and should act towards one another in a spirit of brotherhood*

On the way to the custody facility, David was beaten. Torture was used against him in the van. Two police officers escorting him to the custody tortured David. Can you understand how a husband, a father of three children registered in the Swedish system can be just be victim of violence? Having him beaten on the way to the custody corroborates once again that David's life was meaningless for both police officers. David was told not to talk on the phone to his wife when she was calling him to have information about where to be kept in custody. Police officers harassed him and told him if he speaks to his wife he will be beaten. He was even told to be killed. Both police officers emphasize that they would not care about his death. Words that police officers threw on the face of the applicant violated the human rights. The rights of David were useless. The applicant did not have any right anymore. Meanwhile, there is the right of prisoners and the right of aliens. All these are not existent for David since he is about to be sent to the custody. Actually, all these concerned questions of torture and inhuman or degrading treatment. Following this, the head of family was even unjustly accused for drug issues when incarcerated in Märsta. In view of this, both the immigration service and the police plotted against David for him to be charged and deported.

It was said of David not to continually be kept in custody since he was about to be released. To have intentionally kept David in custody corroborates structural discrimination against the applicant. To be kept in custody signifies David who has a permanent work is no longer willing to exercise as an employee. He was therefore cut off from earning his life and supporting his family. The family business that David created run up debts since the productivity that was rendered by the applicant is no longer able because of being kept in custody. Once the family company runs up debts the business automatically closes. Neither David Kayode nor Johanna Granered-Ogundedji could afford managing the debts. David was therefore reported to the debt collection service when being kept in custody. Not pleased with the incarceration of David and the closure of his family company the combined unit of police and immigration services plotted to have David arrested for him to spend more than eleven months in custody. This signifies that both combined unit wanted David to spend additional months over than the eleven others he already spent unfairly in custody. For the system to have control and right over the applicant strategies consisting in having charged with drug was an option. Once charged with drug, this would seem to be an adequate expression of law.

In this view, the applicant would have lawfully been charged and kept in custody and later deported. Despite of the plot David was filled with vigilance and outmaneuvered the enemy. He required investigations and the case to be prosecuted. He won the case without being compensated. Lack of compensation confirms the plot. The actions were then planned for David to be sent back to Africa, since a decision ordering his exclusion for two years was issued by both the immigration service and the border police. Both administrations were keen to fulfill what they decided though it goes against the law. Structural discrimination against the applicant and his family was corroborated throughout the processing period. Why did these bodies wished in every circumstance to deport the applicant when he is eligible?

Johanna Granered- Ogundedji once went to the immigration service in Sundbyberg (Stockholm) and requires her husband's residence permit to the immigration officers. The actions by Johanna displeased these officers since they considered Mrs Ogundedji's reaction bold actions. This action may explain the reason why David's residence permit application was rejected even though he was eligible. The reaction of Mrs Ogundedji that was considered bold actions would have never impacted the decision to be taken concerning the application of David Kayode Ogundedji.

These are two diametrically opposed feelings. Administrations have to make logical decisions and not being based on overly sensitive reactions. Immigration officers are neither in any relationship nor with David and Johanna. What they have to do is to study the case and find out if David fulfills or not the requirements of an applicant in search for residence permit in Sweden. This is where their tasks are limited to administrative functions and not expand over dimensions which are nothing to do with logical positions. The reaction of Johanna was fair since she wants her family to be united or unified than being dispersed because she was waiting for a baby.

The reaction neither constitutes an offence nor a crime. The baby she expects to give birth to was the first born with David. She is not experienced in taking care of the baby alone. She wishes to be assisted by her husband. Seeing the dramatic situation of her husband and the days of delivery close, she fears loosing control. No child needs to be taken care of with the assistance of only one of the parents. Each child needs the presence of both the parents. Scientific research confirms that children with both parents have a good quality education.[50]

[50] G. R. Burgio & John D. Lantos, *Primum non nocere today*, Elsevier, Amsterdam, 1998, p.149-151

Presence of both parents promotes self- confidence and has a positive overall effect on children environment.[51] Actually, children with both parents are psychologically and physically stable than the ones with one or no parent(s). To have acted in such a way, immigration officers would have then understood that Johanna and David relationship is a true one. Investigations conducted for eligible applicant to be issued residence permit is confirmed and corroborated through Johanna's reaction and pregnancy. Immigration officers' investigations were then fully completed based on the reaction Mrs Ogundedji showed to them when she visited their office in Sundbyberg (Stockholm). Johanna's reaction talked more than words. Actually, Johanna's reaction would have never constituted a reason for punishing her husband. She did what she could to show compassion to her husband who suffers from injustice and mistreatment. All normal and sensitive women, wives and mothers would have reacted as experienced by Johanna Granered- Ogundedji. The relationship of David and Johanna was a true one as mentioned in the Swedish immigration law related to applicants in need of residence permit.

---

[51] Shane J. Lopez & C. R. Snyder, *The Oxford handbook of positive psychology*, Oxford Library of Psychology, Oxford, 2011, p.550-555

Neither David nor his family needed to be victims of the coalition immigration service- police- and debt collection. To have intentionally separated David from his family and to deport him from Sweden to Africa signifies that the combined unit (immigration and police) violated the Convention on the Rights of the Child since they did not care about the special safeguards and care the children need as mentioned by the United Nations (UN).[52] They committed crime since the three children of David Kayode Ogundedji were under the age of eighteen (18). Daniela, Gabriela and Izak were born in 2017, 2020 and 2021 respectively. They are all covered by the law when their father was unfairly suffering from injustice and mistreatment. However, a question may have been raised in such a way that people could doubt about the paternity of these children. There is no doubt here to emphasize that the children are not David's kids. There is an attestation of paternity that supports the legal right of these children to be David's ones. At this level there is no doubt and the debate concerning paternity is closed.

---

[52] United Nations, Convention on the Rights of the Child, Adopted on November 20, 1989 by the General Assembly resolution 44/25, Preamble, Article 1 *"For the purposes of the present Convention, a child means every human being below the age of eighteen years unless under the law applicable to the child, majority is attained earlier"*

This kind of injustice and mistreatment the immigration service and police usually applied to eligible applicant has destroyed many family lives and the life of children. The sequestrated parents are for the most fathers. These ones are generally from Africa. Métis children are currently those suffering from injustice intentionally created by the combined unit. Parents (men) that are not psychologically and physically strong abandon their children. At the end, Métis children such as the one of the family Ogundedji are left alone and are left behind. Up till today many are these children who suffer deep psychological issues because of trauma-related problems. How many children under the age of eighteen whether Métis or from other nations are not concerned with this issue which becomes a heavy burden for the state that needs to cover medical expenditures? As demonstrated and confirmed by scientific research and reports worldwide Sweden is one of the most dangerous European states in terms of arm violence. Roots of high risk of gun violence are at the same time political, economical and social. Once these children whose parents have been deported are psychologically affected they get automatically weak and become a new source of delinquency. And this is what the family Ogundedji fights against for their children not to be outcasts in the Swedish civil society.

Somehow the family Ogundedji tries in advance to bring her contribution in order to reduce violence in Sweden. How come these authorities do not stop violating both national and international laws when the end is costly to the state? The process is ongoing since the government or Swedish politicians do not know anything about the violation of laws. This time the family Ogundedji would like to rewrite the story of those who were victims of the system and could not do anything for all kinds of illegal and inhuman actions of both the immigration service and the police to be exposed nationally and internationally. Injustice and mistreatment were applied therefore to both David and his family. Both national and international laws are violated in terms of the father, the mother and the children. It was not an offence that is committed unless a serious crime that needs to be prosecuted either nationally or regionally. In this regards, immigration, police and debt collection officers have to be fair when it comes to exercise their responsibilities. Oaths need to be respected only as have been sworn in. To deny residence permit to an applicant who fulfills the requirements of the immigration laws, is a crime against humanity. This inhuman act necessitates strict and unanimous condemnation. The coalition needs to be prosecuted either in Sweden or in Strasbourg at the European Court of Human Rights (ECHR). David and his family are unlawfully accused and judged.

Injustice and mistreatment applied on David is not ended even though he is nowadays in Sweden since he has only been issued a temporary residence permit. Having had a temporary residence permit confirms that the suffering of the family Ogundedji is postponed since there is a high risk of reconduction of injustice and mistreatment whenever the combined unit wants.

No matter what David worked and paid taxes over years his life seems to be an eternal restarting. David can still endure suffering. When David suffers injustice and mistreatment it is the entire family Ogundedji that is physically and psychologically affected in a negative way. The situation the family went through previously has negatively impacted the second born of the family Ogundedji. Gabriela until today meaning at the age of two cannot speak out. The situation is caused because she suffers trauma. The traumatic reactions she experienced give her no chance just as children learn to speak language very quickly, easily and well. The issue of Gabriela confirms hundred percent that her father, David Kayode Ogundedji, suffered injustice and mistreatment. Gabriela has been negatively impacted and this can be corroborated by a picture (refer to appendix) where she was crying and the situation in which she found itself as a little lovely girl. She suffered with both her parents.

Today, there is no doubt that Gabriela cannot speak but she tries to show signs of happiness since she has both of her parents by her side. Signs of happiness Gabriela shows today have a clear comprehension. She is overwhelmed by the enthusiasm of their parents and her brother Izak and her sister Daniela who frequently comes on week ends and holidays. The most remarquable aspect here is that the youngest son of the family, Izak Ogundedji starts to speak out and walk. Izak is the happier child in the family since he eats and grows well and is also calm. He is a child full of life and joy. Why does Izak show more signs of happiness in comparison with its elder sisters? The difference is clear since the family is unified once again. At the time the father was kept in custody, the son was not born yet and Izak has the opportunity to meet its father for a while before he was deported from Sweden to Benin. As for the young child its father was certainly in holidays. Later, the mother decided with them to visit the dad and they therefore travelled to Africa where they stayed for three months. The two different worlds in which Izak evolves make the child to benefit from its life experience and the empathy gotten from the diverse populations. As a child the mother and the sister visited the father in Africa. Human warmth and affection received in Africa allow the young kid to be happy with itself, other and the nature.

The environment helps Izak to be different from its older siblings. In sum, for children to have it better requires harmony, affection and empathy in the environment they evolve. When Izak was born the situation of the father seemed to have been calm even though this is not a reality. The truth behind this was that the period was not disturbed. Izak is luckier than Daniela and Gabriela. Both the older siblings were not then as lucky as the younger brother is today. We hope that the presence of the father in Sweden will continuously stimulate and improve the level of joy of both Daniela and Gabriela to reach more or less the one of the brother. All these parameters have to be taken into consideration for the combined unit not to create deliberately additional issues concerning the permanent residence permit of David Kayode Ogundedji who is once again back to Sweden after a period of tragedy, injustice and mistreatment.

## *In custody*

Anyone incarcerated or kept in custody has right to fair treatment since there are basic laws of prisoners. This law has been adopted on December 1990 by the General Assembly resolution 45/111 and concerns basic principles for the treatment of prisoners. The law stipulates that "*All prisoners shall be treated with respect due to their inherent dignity and value as human beings.*

*There shall be no discrimination on the grounds of race, colour, sex, language, religion, political or other opinion, national or social origin, property, birth or other status".* [53] In the case such laws are existent and David has been unfairly condemned over years for reasons of residence permit application, then we may question ourselves if these laws are for special groups of peoples or concern all human beings living on the planet earth. If these laws have to be applied to all human beings and David suffers injustice and mistreatment, then these laws protect a certain group of people and condemn others. Actually, this is not the reason for which these laws are ratified. They are ratified to ensure that all human beings are cover by the laws. Despite of this some European states for which the theory of classification of human races is advantaged denied the rights of other residence permit applicants to be mistreated. The case of David is typical evidence among many others illustrating the inhuman actions of both the immigration service and police. To be kept in custody and currently be victim of human rights violation, David's life was not safe. This a true reality since the detainee got sick of corona for a period of time. He was in a very critical health condition. David's life depended on the Swedish authorities since they detained him in custody.

---

[53] United Nations, Human rights, *Basic principles for the treatment of prisoners*, General Assembly resolution 45/11, December 14, 1990

To be responsible of the life of a detainee requires attention. The sort of attention David was supposed to get from the Swedish authorities has to be special. In view of what happened to the detainee, it could be said of the Swedish authorities to endanger the life of David no matter what he was a residence permit applicant or not. He was treated as a criminal while he is not. What the combined unit was after was to condemn the detainee with offences or crimes so that he could be legally detained after the decided period of incarceration. Following this, the applicant was falsely accused of detaining drug when he has nothing to do with narcotic. All these accusations have to come to pass so that David should be kept for an additional detention when he has the right to be freed from custody. Abuse of power, harassment, violence and false accusations were currently used against the father and husband applicant. Scientific research demonstrates that people regularly stressed with the abovementioned inhuman actions are the subject of high level of psychological disease and distress. Having had David encountered with psychological and physiological stressors would have caused him huge health damage. David was therefore damaged both physically and psychologically when kept in custody. The situation affected the detainee's appetite which prevents him from eating more conveniently. David remains with no food over weeks.

Not eating at all leads to the loss calories. Loss of calories affects the body and finally the health of the detainee. The detainee lost drastically weight since no protein could be found in his body. David suffered accusation, mistreatment and injustice when incarcerated in Märsta. In sum, the basic principles for the treatment of prisoners were violated in the case of the detainee when kept in custody. No matter what David did or not for good or wrong the combined unit wanted him weak, dead or alive when deportation from Sweden to Benin would occur. Let us think about the way Davis is treated while he is not a criminal? How a criminal is then treated compared with a residence permit applicant? David suffers awfully hard. Here we consider that David is a victim of human rights violation. The violation he experienced is more than the word itself since it goes beyond the mistreatment of what can be said to be considered a violation. There is no word that can qualify this inhuman action applied to David and his family. To see an applicant whose wife gave birth to the first child of the couple and the woman has no experience of taking care of a baby going up and down between the combined unit in order for her to see her husband released from custody since he is eligible for residence permit application.

In view of the situation of the woman no chance was given to her husband to join her since her coming in and coming out confirm that both of them are in a true relationship. No matter what effort the wife did the fallacious decision of the immigration office was never changed on behalf of the applicant who suffers human rights violation over months from December 2019 to April 2021. To survive such a mistreatment can be said of the applicant to be a hero. David survived high-level mistreatment. The only remaining thing that David suffers today vertebral column pain since he has been beaten bloody in the van when taken to the camp facility in Märsta.

David and his family lost everything they have that could lead to a better life. Today, the reunified family, the husband, the wife and the children, all together hope for a new start since they have confidence in the father and good husband to do his level best and work harder and get back once again what they lost due to the combined unit. The family is nowadays happy and even happier than ever since all of them live under the same roof. Only Daniela goes and comes back whenever she wants, during week-ends and when she feels like being with her mother-in-law, her junior sister and brother as well as her dad. Daniela is loved by Johanna as her own mother since both Johanna and Daniela had good relationship when she was a little baby.

Regardless of the trauma created by the combined unit (immigration service and police), all members of the family Ogundedji are more than strong enough to maintain the connection for a more robust new life. This can be considered a victory upon the immigration service and police which decided to destroy an entire family life. How can people's wish consists in destroying other persons family life when they have their own family life to take care of. Should that make sense? No, that is not the plan of God for human beings. God's purpose is that all populations live a peaceful life worldwide. And this is the purpose for which He created heaven and earth and filled it with human beings. Those going against the will of God under the cover of administrations have to be fair and also fear God. The fear of God is where life starts. To wish to stop someone's family life and build up once own family is impossible. Otherwise, those trying to destroy other peoples' family life are individuals who do not have any family member. These ones may be easily jealous of people who are making it in life. And this can be the reason why David was alienated and suffers violence, injustice and mistreatment. David did not need to be kept in custody and separated from his family. He deserves more than that. He was supposed to be issued a residence permit since he is eligible.

He therefore needs to be compensated for suffering injustice and mistreatment with his family. In the case the combined unit considers the different relationship of David to be the reason for which he has to suffer injustice and mistreatment, we are diametrically oppose to this and reject this assumption.

## *The relationships*

David once in Sweden met his first wife with whom he got married in 2014. When the first marriage collapsed he was a couple with Sandrine Lukula with whom he got his first daughter, Daniela Ogundedji. In view of the complicated situation with the parents of his girl-friend, David decided to be in a safe relationship and this is when he met Johanna Granered- Ogundedji. David and Johanna are married in august 2019. In sum, David has had three relationships with three children. The three children are those of the last two relationships. To have been in three relationships with three different ladies does not make of David a womanizer. In Sweden, divorce is not sacred since women divorce easily. Women for the most do not give more attention to marriage or relationship. In view of this, David became a victim of his first wife who got tied to a drug addict. Drug addiction is not an option that can be accepted in Sweden.

To have informed the immigration service about the drug issue, the administration used the situation against him to have him later kept in custody. Did David do wrong in informing the immigration service about the issue of drug that his former wife was addicted to? To use drug addiction denunciation against David to deport him from Sweden is anything that can only be promoted by people who themselves are drug addicts or those wishing to destroy Swedish civilians' life. To have inform the immigration service about the issue of drug should have determine the life of David. This may have confirmed the type of person David is. The applicant is a correct person who does not deal with narcotics. The attitude of David rejected the prejudice of the combined unit concerning certain groups of people, especially Africans, to whom the applicant may belong to. Mostly, Africans are considered to deal with drug and this is a prejudice. Once David is African and did not deal with drugs, this put the combined unit to fall into a fit of rage. Actually, the denunciation of drug addiction broke down prejudices. David wanted to save the life of his children-in-law, whose mother brought home someone with whom they consume drugs in front of the kids. The denunciation should have been anything to be saluted; otherwise David became a victim of both the immigration service and his former wife.

He was confronted with the boy-friend of his former wife in association with the combined unit. This attitude did not stop the applicant from fighting for his residence permit. To be conformed with the required documents of eligibility, the applicant had a girl-friend who already was waiting for a baby and later a wife. During the process of being issued residence permit the applicant did what was in power to conform himself to the Swedish Act concerning the eligibility of residence permit. David did nothing wrong to suffer injustice and mistreatment unless tried to be conformed hundred percent to the Act concerning immigrants. To have had a child with Sandrine Lukula and later been married to Johanna did not make of the applicant anyone who did not know what to do or want. The situation of his parents-in-law makes him to leave Sandrine, the mother of his first born daughter, Daniela Ogundedji, for Johanna Granered-Ogundedji with whom he got married in 2019. Out of the three ladies the applicant met, Johanna was the one who he did not have problem with and on top of that the parents of his new wife love him better than those of Sandrine Lukula. So, nothing in his third relation could stop him from being loved. He loves his wife, Johanna and she loves him back. The kind of love they experienced is the true one since there was no tragedy in it in comparison with the first two ones in which drug addiction and parents-in-law were implicated.

The love with Johanna is the perfect one. Johanna even confirms it when she visited the facility of the immigration service once she met the case officers in charge of the application. The determination of Johanna spoke more than words. Her presence should have determined the residence permit to be issued to David. Not only her determination but her relationship with Daniela, the first born of the Ogundedji and even the pregnancy she beard then were strong evidences. All evidences were gathered for David to be issued residence permit and not be deported from Sweden to Benin. The different relationships of David should have never constituted any excuses for the combined unit to deny and deport illegally David from Sweden after being victim of injustice and mistreatment. To have acted in such a way against the applicant consists of the violation of human rights and fundamental freedoms. Regardless of the problem that broke between the parents of Sandrine and David, the girl-friend of the applicant has good relationship with her former boy-friend and his new wife, Johanna Granered- Ogundedji. Three of them are good friends and this is the reason why Sandrine has nothing against Johanna to regularly take Daniela with her. Daniela was even more attached to Johanna than her own mother, Sandrine. All these signs are strong enough for the immigration service to issue residence permit to the applicant.

Instead of being issued residence permit force is used on the applicant and riddled with accusations from the first beginning to the end. In sum, it is then confirmed here that the two last relationships of David weighed more than the first one. In this case, the first one cannot destroy the two last ones since they are more important and safer than the one related to drug issue. David has a clean record since he has never been convicted. He pays taxes when he worked and even created a family company from which he employs workers and paid additional taxes. David is good for the Swedish civil society since he contributed to its growth and success. He brings additional contribution. He is not a burden to the Swedish state. He has his own apartment, a work and a company and denounces drug issue. All these make of the applicant to be a person who integrated the Swedish system. To be integrated in a civil society and not being treated correctly by authorities suppose to intervene with fairness and ethics and morals confirms that injustice and mistreatment are methods that have been administered to the applicant. Actually, the different relationships may have never impacted in a wrong way the issuing of residence permit to the applicant since he fulfills the requirements of the Act of immigration.

The two last relationships were sufficient for David to be left alone with his family and issued residence permit than being taken away from his beautiful children and sad wife. Justice needs therefore to be done for David and his family. They have to be compensated for all injustice and mistreatment they experienced during the last three years, meaning from 2019 to 2022. The case of the family Ogundedji which is known by journalists has to be dispatched all around Sweden and worldwide so that justice can prevail over injustice and mistreatment. No one has to suffer injustice and mistreatment for matter of skin color or gender and social class. David has to be compensated and issued permanent residence permit since he is eligible since then. The Swedish Act of immigration emphasizes that anyone who is in a serious relationship with a Swedish citizen after a two years period has to be issued a permanent residence permit. Johanna and David lived together before being married even though it seemed than they were not registered at the same address. They lived together for a good period before they got married. To have kept David in custody and later deported him from Sweden does counsel the two years period. The combined unit did it on purpose for the Act of immigration not to concern the applicant who suffers injustice and mistreatment. The two years period allow David to be issued a permanent residence permit is valid for the applicant.

If being forced to be kept in custody and deported is synonymous to have not spent two years with Johanna, this has to be rejected since the couple was currently in contact regardless of the situation. Johanna regularly visited David in custody. In the case that was not possible so Johanna would have never given birth to Izak Ogundedji who is born in 2021. So, this option of saying of Johanna and David not to have been living together for a two years period is anything to be considered otherwise it has to be rejected. The family Ogundedji lived together for two years. No matter what kind of gymnastic that was performed by the immigration service and the police to issue a two years residence permit which is a temporary one to the applicant goes against the rights of the applicant. It goes against the rights of the applicant since he is denied a permanent residence permanent while he is eligible for it. To issue a permanent residence permit to David Ogundedji is not a weakness for both the immigration service and the police unless a wise decision to be respected. The family Ogundedji needs to be stressed once again since injustice and mistreatment are still possible since the father and husband is always in the collimator of the combined unit. No addition drama has to be planned against the family Ogundedji who continually suffers post-trauma caused by the immigration service and the police that applied injustice and mistreatment against the applicant and family members.

# CONCLUSION

David as a former police officer and native of Benin emigrated to Europe in 2013. He first travelled to Germany and his final destination Sweden. Once in Sweden he met a native of the country with whom hc got married to in Benin after periods of tribulation in the land. David was falsely accused of drug issues of which he was found no guilty and compensated. His life in Sweden was a complete mess since he has been kept in custody randomly regardless of the fact that he regularly paid taxes between 6000 to 7000 Swedish crowns monthly. During his stay in Sweden, David had had three different relationships. When the first one collapsed from whom he got no child he met an African lady named Sandrine Lukula. David has three children from two different mothers. His first born Daniela Ogundedji came to life in 2017 while Gabriela and Isak were born between 2020 and 2021 respectively. David as a workaholic, a good father and husband suffered strong sense of injustice. Not only that he is a victim of injustice unless he was seriously mistreated by the two police officers. The system makes him and his family company to run up debts. David is both victim of injustice and mistreatment. At the regional level since the deportation happens with the conspiracy of the French consulate in Benin.

Injustice and mistreatment will always happens in Sweden due to other Europeans involment in the inhuman actions. The case of police violence reported by his wife Johanna Granered- Ogundedji for deliberate assault and intentionally bodily harm, on December 10, 2022 to the police station of Kungsholmen was dismissed not later than two days after, on December 15, 2022 (refer to attachment in appendix). The family Ogundedji is still processing the case of police violence and residence permit as well as the one of the collection debt service for justice to be done on behalf of her dear husband. Johanna Granered- Ogundedji is dedicated to present the case to the regional court, the European Court for human rights (ECHR). Having violated the Universal Declaration of Human Rights means no excuses for the Swedish immigration body and the police as well as the debt collection service. In view of this, justice has to be done for the respect of human rights and fundamental freedoms. Perpetrators of violence, injustice and mistreatment have to be prosecuted and charged with both an offence and a crime. For justice to prevail over injustice, the combined unit has to be brought before a judge or the relevant judiciary authorities.

In the case that injustice would not be condemned by social justice then God whose purpose for human being is to live a peaceful life will plead the cause of the weak and poor and plunder the soul of those who plunder then according to the Holy Scriptures.[54]

The answer to the research question mentioned previously, we can confirm with confidence that David suffers injustice, mistreatment and deportation due to his skin color and his wife Johanna Granered- Ogundedji's intervention. Her action was considered a challenge for the case officers in charge of the application of her husband. Alone, these immigration officers were not strong enough to defeat the family Ogundedji. They associate therefore the border police and the debt collection officers to their fight against the Ogundedji to be won on their behalf. Having done all that were in their power to use force on David Kayode Ogundedji, to mistreat him and to make him a victim of human rights violation, the family Ogundedji is in the end victorious since the applicant is back regardless of the period of residence permit that was issued to the head of family. We are aware that the fight is not over but it can be corroborated that the Ogundedji's are both psychologically and physically strong no matter what the family members were negatively affected by the inhuman actions of the combined unit.

---

[54] New King James Version, Proverbs 22:23

Probably the worst will come to pass and this is the reason why the family is alerting the entire world about the case of David Kayode Ogundedji to be followed up by international organizations, associations, activists and adjuvants of human rights and fundamental freedoms.

The response to the problematic is that it is not all applicants who fulfill the requirements of the Swedish Act of immigration that are issued residence permit no matter they are eligible. Residence permit is issued differently depending on the case officer, certain aspects and other prerequisites. What can be concluded is that residence permit issuing in Sweden is currently contradicting the Act of immigration. More than half of the applicants' cases are handled with injustice and violation of human rights.

The opening question is the following: When will the Swedish immigration service handle residence permit applications with fairness and ethics and morals?

Page intentionally left blank

# BIBLIOGRAPHY

## General books

Aleksandra Djurasovic, *Ideology, political transitions and the city: The case of Mostar, Bosnia and Herzegovina*, Routledge, London & New York, 2016

Amartya Kumar Sen Lamont, *The idea of Justice*, The Belknap Press of Harvard University Press, Cambridge, Massachusetts, 2009

Andreas Frank, *Committed sensations, An initiation to homosexuality: The gay & lesbian*, handbook & compendium on coming-out & same- sex partnerships, Nordersted, 2020

Audry Berman, Shirlee J. Snyder & Barbara Kozier, *Kozier & Erb's fundamentals of nursing Australian edition*, Pearson, Melbourne, 2014

Ben Akpan & Teresa J. Kennedy, *Science education in theory and practice: An introductory guide to learning theory*, Springer, Cham, 2000

Ben Laurence, *Agents of change, Political philosophy in practice*, Harvard University Press, Cambridge, Massachusetts, 2021

Bernard A. Cook, *Europe since 1945, An Encyclopedia, Volume II*, Garland Publishing, Inc., New York & London, 2001

Bruce A. Thyer, *The handbook of social work research methods*, Sage Publications, Inc., London, 2001

Bruce Barton, Philip Comfort, Grant Osborne, Linda K. Taylor & Dave Veerman, *Life application New Testament commentary*, Tyndale House Publishers, Inc., Illinois, 2016

Craig A. Williams & David V. James, *Science for exercise and sport*, Routledge, London & New York, 2001

Daurius Figueira, *Cocaine and heroin trafficking in the Caribbean, Volume 2*, iUniverse, Inc., New York, Lincoln & Shanghai, 2006

Dinesh Bhugra, *Oxford textbook of migrant psychiatry*, Oxford University Press, Oxford, 2021

Dr Ley G. Ikpo, *Cour pénale internationale: Injustice ou pas contre Charles Blé Goudé, De 2002 à 2022*, Kindle Direct Publishing, Washington, 2022

Eleni Kosta, Ronald Leenes & Irene Kamara, *Research handbook on EU data protection law*, Edward Elgar Publishing, Inc., Cheltenham & Massachusetts, 2022

Erik Proper, Marc Lankhordt & Marten Schönherr, *Trends in enterprise architecture research: 5th workshop*, Springer, New York, 2010

G. R. Burgio & John D. Lantos, *Primum non nocere today*, Elsevier, Amsterdam, 1998

George Sher, *Ethics: Essential readings in moral theory*, Routledge, London, 2012

Georges Guille-Escuret, *Structures sociales et systèmes naturels, l'assemblage scientifique est-il réalisable?* ISTE Editions, London, 2018

Gregory Feist & Michael Gorman, *Handbook of the psychology of science*, Springer, Publishing Company, New York, 2013

Guttorm Flostad, *Philosophy of Justice, Springer*, New York & London, 2014

James A. Marcum, *An introductory philosophy of medicine: Humanizing modern medicine*, Springer, New Jersey, 2008

Jean NcNiff & Jack Whitehead, *All you need to know about action research*, SAGE, London, 2006

Jeanne H. Ballantine & Joan Z. Spade, *Schools and societies, A sociological approach to education*, SAGE, California & London, 2015

Jean-Philipp Dr. Deranty, *Beyond communication, A critical study of Axel Honneth's*, BRILL, Leiden & Boston, 2009

Jeremy M. Smallwood, *The ESD control program handbook*, Wiley & Sons Ltd, New Jersey, 2020

John Rawls, *A theory of justice, Revised edition*, The Belknap Press of Harvard University Press, Cambridge, Massachusetts, 1995

Kofi Kissi Dompere, *The theory of knowledge square: The fuzzy rational foundations of the knowledge-production systems*, Springer, New York, 2012

Mahendra Lawoti, *Towards a democratic Nepal: Inclusive political institutions*, Sage Publications, New Delhi & London, 2005

Malcolm Payne & Emma Reith-Hall, *The Routledge Handbook of social work theory*, Oxon & New York, Routledge International Handbooks, 2019

Marc Jacquemain, *Le sens du juste: cadre normative et usages sociaux des critères de justice*, Les Éditions de l'Université de Liège, Liège, 2005

Miriam Yvette Vega, *Relational schemas and condom-use in heterosexual relationships*, University of California, Berkeley, 1999

National science Foundation, *Summaries of projects completed*, National Science foundation, 1979

N. Sullivan & L. Mitchell D. Goodman, *Social work with groups: Social justice through personal, community, and societal change*, Routledge, New York & London, 2013

Paul Tannery, *Recherches sur l'histoire de l'astronomie ancienne*, Cambridge University Press, Cambridge, 2015

Ralph Griffiths & George Edward Griffiths, The monthly review, Volume 65, London, 1781, p.203-207

Richard K. Gardiner, *Treaty interpretation*, Oxford University Press, Oxford, 2015

Robert Koulish, *Immigration and American democracy: Subverting the rule of law*, Routledge, New York & London, 2010

Shaun P. Young, *Reflections on Rawls: An assessment of his legacy*, Routledge, London & New York, 2016

Sergej Flere & Rudy Klanjek, *The rise and fall of socialist Yugoslavia: Elite nationalism and the collapse of a federation*, Lexington books, Lanham, Boulder, New York & London, 2019

Shane J. Lopez & C. R. Snyder, *The Oxford handbook of positive psychology*, Oxford Library of Psychology, Oxford, 2011

Sigmund Gronmo, *Social research methods: Qualitative, quantitative and mixed methods approaches*, SAGE, London, Singapore & New Delhi 2019

Simon Adams, *History of the world (e-book)*, Dorling Kindersley Limited, London, New York & Munich, 2004

Sven Ove Hansson & Gertrude Hirsh Hadorn, *The argument turn in policy analysis: Reasoning about uncertainty*, Springer, Cham, 2016

Statens Offentliga Utredningar, Sverige, Utredningen om tillsynen inom socialtjänst, SOU 2007: 082 *Samordnad och tydlig tillsyn av socialtjänsten*, Edita Sverige AB, Stockhom, 2007

Swanee Hunt, *Worlds apart: Bosnian lessons for global security*, Duke University Press, Durham & London, 2011

Terri Givens, Gary P. Freeman & David L. Leal, *Immigration policy and security: US, European, and Commonwealth perspectives*, Routledge, London & New York, 2008

Thomas Pogge, *Realizing Rawls*, Cornell University press, Ithaca & London, 1989

Torion Kent, *Love yesterday, today and future tomorrows: Inspiration through notes, music and quotes*, 365 Love Publishing, USA, 2013

Vidya Dhar Mahajan, *Political theory*, S. Chand & Company Ltd, New Delhi, 2006

United States, Congress House, Committee on Foreign Affairs, Subcommittee on Asian and Pacific Affairs, *Human Rights in Asia: Noncommunist countries*, U.S government Printing Office, Washington. D.C, 1980

Yves Lenoir  & Alessandra Froelich, *La reconnaissance à l'école: Les perspectives internationales*, Presse de l'Université Laval, Québec, 2016

Zvi Gitelman, *The new Jewish diaspora: Russian- speaking immigrants in the United States, Israel, and Germany*, Rutgers, The State University, New Jersey, 2016

## Articles

Mark Zanin & Cheng Xiao, *The public health response to the Covid-19 outbreak in mainland China: A narrative review*, Journal of thoracic disease, Vol 12, No 8 (August 2020)

Philippe Adair, *La théorie de la justice de John Rawls, Contrat social versus utilitarisme*, Revue francaise de la science politique/ Année 1991/ 41-1/ pp.81-96, p.81

Sveriges Riksdag, *En ny hälso- och sjukvårdslag, Socialutskottets betänkande 2016/17 SooU5*

United Nations, Convention on the Rights of the Child, Adopted on November 20, 1989 by the General Assembly resolution 44/25, Preamble, Article 1 *"For the purposes of the present Convention, a child means every human being below the age of eighteen years unless under the law applicable to the child, majority is attained earlier"*

United Nations, Human rights, *Basic principles for the treatment of prisoners*, General Assembly resolution 45/11, December 14, 1990

United Nations, Universal Declaration of Human Rights, Preamble, Article 1: *All human beings are born free and equal in dignity and rights. They are endowed with reason and conscience and should act towards one another in a spirit of brotherhood*

Uppehållstillstånd får beviljas efter inresan om utlänningen har stark anknyting till en person som är bosatt I Sverige och det inte skäligen kan krävas att utlänningen återvänder till ett annat land för att ge in ansökan där

## Newspapers

Aftonbladet, Söderhamn, *Försvunne treåringen i Ljusne hittad död*, Publicerad den 8 juni 2022, kl 19:00, av Jesefine Karlsson, Amanda Hälsten, Fanny Westling & Oskar Forsberg

# Appendix

## Annex 1: Johanna & David Ogundedji's wedding day

# Annex 2: David beaten by the two police officers shows wound on lips

# Annex 3: Medical certificate from an authorized doctor when the applicant arrived at the detention facility wounded by the two police officers

Rapport från sjukvården

| Datum: 19.12.12 | Avd: 3 | Rapporterat av: Bea |
|---|---|---|
| Allmän Info: | | |

Namn: Kayode David Ogundedji

| Dossié nr: | Reserv nr: | Född: 861125-1292 |
|---|---|---|

Bedömning av åtgärd:

Smärta i kroppen efter omild behandling.
Fått Alvedon brus och Ibuprofen att ha i sitt
skåp att ta v.b.

Utskriven medicin: —

| Namn: | | |
|---|---|---|
| Dossié nr: | Reserv nr: | Född: |

Bedömning av åtgärd:

Utskriven medicin:

| Namn: | | |
|---|---|---|
| Dossié nr: | Reserv nr: | Född: |

Bedömning av åtgärd:

# Annex 4: Case reported on December 10, 2022 and dismissed on December 15, 2022 (2 pages)

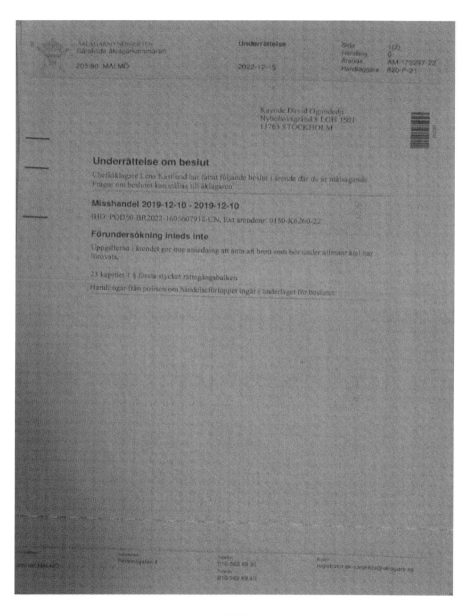

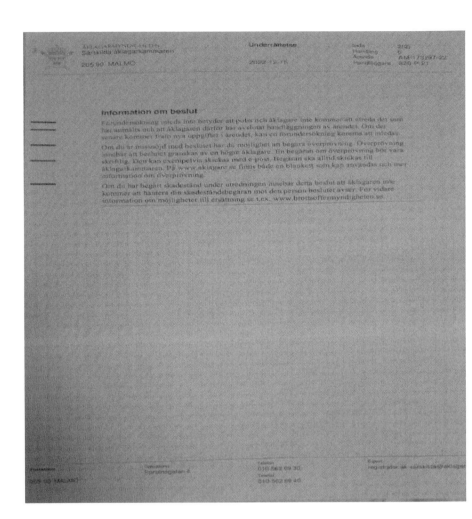

ÅKLAGARMYNDIGHETEN
Särskilda åklagarkammaren

205 90 MALMÖ

Underrättelse

2022-12-16

Sida 2(2)
Handling 5
Ärende AM-173297-22
Handläggare 930-11-21

## Information om beslut

Förundersökning inleds inte betyder att polis och åklagare inte kommer att utreda det som har anmälts och att åklagaren därför har avslutat handläggningen av ärendet. Om den senare kommer fram nya uppgifter i ärendet, kan en förundersökning komma att inledas.

Om du är missnöjd med beslutet har du möjlighet att begära överprövning. Överprövning innebär att beslutet granskas av en högre åklagare. En begäran om överprövning bör vara skriftlig. Den kan exempelvis skickas med e-post. Begäran ska alltid skickas till åklagarkammaren. På www.aklagare.se finns både en blankett som kan användas och mer information om överprövning.

Om du har begärt skadestånd under utredningen innebär detta beslut att åklagaren inte kommer att hantera din skadeståndsbegäran mot den person beslutet avser. För vidare information om möjligheter till ersättning se t.ex. www.brottsoffermyndigheten.se.

Postadress
205 90 MALMÖ

Gatuadress
Ingenjörsgatan 4

Telefon
010-562 09 30

Telefax
010-562 09 40

E-post
registrator.ak-sarskilda@aklagare

2/2

# Annex 5: Plot for deportation of the applicant when still kept unlawfully in custody

**Arkiverad:** den 3 september 2020 11:04:23
**Från:** Registrator Attunda Tingsrätt - TAA
**Skickat:** den 3 september 2020 11:01:49
**Till:** TAA - Enhetsbrevlåda Brottmålsenhet
**Ämne:** VB: Planerad huvudförhandling
**Svar krävs:** Nej
**Precision:** Normal

ATTUNDA TINGSRÄTT
Översändes för kännedom

B 6310-20

Med vänlig hälsning

**Ghertie Noe Fredes**
Domstolshandläggare, Beredningsavdelning, Samordningsenhet, Attunda tingsrätt
08-561 695 43 • ghertie.noefredes@dom.se • Attunda tingsrätts webbd

Så behandlar vi personuppgifter

**Från:** mattias.halin@polisen.se <mattias.halin@polisen.se>
**Skickat:** den 3 september 2020 10:53
**Till:** Registrator Attunda Tingsrätt - TAA <attunda.tingsratt@dom.se>
**Ämne:** Planerad huvudförhandling

Hej

Jag handlägger ett ärendet gällande utvisning av en person som även har en planerad huvudförhandling hos er den 9 oktober 2020.

Med anledning av att han sitter i förvar för att vi ska kunna verkställa utvisningen undrar jag om det finns någon möjlighet att tidigarelägga den huvudförhandlingen? Om den möjligheten inte finns kan det bli så att vi är tvungna att släppa honom ur förvar.

Personen i fråga: David Ogundedji, 19861125-1292. Åklagarmyndighetens dnr. AM-67554-20. Gränspolisens dnr. Gällande förvarsfrågan A596.890/2019

Med vänlig hälsning,

**Mattias Halin**
Verkställighetshandläggare
Gränspolisenheten Stockholm

Telefon: 010-563 88 68
utl.stockholm@polisen.se

Polismyndigheten
106 75 Stockholm
Besök: Kungsholmsgatan 37
Telefon till polisen: 114 14

 **Polisen**

Tänk på miljön! Skriv inte ut det här meddelandet om det inte är nödvändigt.

# Annex 6: David illegally accused of drug issue

**Polisen**

Förhör

Signerat av

Signerat datum

| Enhet | Diarienr |
|---|---|
| Polisregion Stockholm, Utredning 1 LPO Sollentuna | 5000-K293008-20 |

| Hörd person | Personnummer |
|---|---|
| Ogundedji, Kayode David | 19861125-1292 |

| Den hörde är | ID Styrkt | Sätt | Ställning till misstänkt - målsägande - vittne |
|---|---|---|---|
| Misstänkt | Ja | Genom personalen på förvaret i Märsta | |

| Tolk | Språk |
|---|---|
| | |

**Brottsmisstanke / Anledning till förhöret**
David Kayode Ogundedji underrättas misstanke om ringa narkotikabrott, innehav genom att genom att han innehaft 1,56 g Cannabisharts i form av bruna bitar samt 3,39 g Cannabisharts i form av torrt växtmaterial Cannabisharts är ett narkotiskt preparat. Detta uppdagades i samband med visitation den 7 mars 2020 i Migrationsverkets lokaler på Maskingatan 4, Arlandastad

| Underrättad om misstanke | Underrättad om rätt till försvarare (best i FUK 12§ lakttagna) | |
|---|---|---|
| Ja | Ja | |

| Försvarare/ombud önskas | Försvarare/ombud närvarande | Godtar den försvarare som rätten förordnar |
|---|---|---|
| | | |

| Förhörsledare | Förhörsdatum | Förhör påbörjat | Förhör avslutat |
|---|---|---|---|
| Katrine Mattsson | 2020-05-08 | 10:00 | 10:28 |

| Förhörsplats | Typ av förhör | Förhörssätt |
|---|---|---|
| PO Nord, Sollentuna | RB 23:6 | Telefonförhör |

| Förhörsvittne | Utskrivet av |
|---|---|
| | KM |

**Berättelse**

*Förhörsledarens (FL) frågor och kommentarer skrivs med kursiv stil*

*David Kayode Ogundedji informeras om sina rättigheter enligt FuK § 12, rätten till försvarare, rätten att inte behöva yttra sig i förhör, rätten till tolk samt rätten till information om utredning och misstanken till viss del.*

*David Kayode Ogundedji underrättas misstanke om ringa narkotikabrott, innehav genom att genom att han innehaft 1,56 g Cannabisharts i form av bruna bitar samt 3,39 g Cannabisharts i form av torrt växtmaterial Cannabisharts är ett narkotiskt preparat. Detta uppdagades i samband med visitation den 7 mars 2020 i Migrationsverkets lokaler på Maskingatan 4, Arlandastad.*

*David förstår vad han är misstänkt för.*

*David Kayode Ogundedij FÖRNEKAR BROTT*

# Annex 7: Case of drug issue dismissed for lack of evidence

2

ATTUNDA TINGSRÄTT  
Avdelning 1

**DOM**  
2020-12-21

Mål nr: B 6310-20

### YRKANDEN M.M.

Åklagaren väckte den 1 juni 2020 åtal mot David Ogundedji för ringa narkotikabrott under följande påstående (5000-K293008-20).

David Ogundedji har olovligen innehaft 4,95 gram cannabisharts, som är narkotika. Det hände den 7 mars 2020 på Migrationsverket Märsta, Maskingatan 4, Arlandastad, Sigtuna kommun. David Ogundedji begick gärningen med uppsåt.

Lagrum: 1 § första stycket, 6 punkten och 2 § narkotikastrafflagen (1968:64)

Åklagaren yrkade vidare att i beslag tagen narkotika jämte emballage skulle förverkas enligt 6 § narkotikastrafflagen, 20020-5000-BG29486.1 och 2.

Åklagaren har nu lagt ned åtalet, eftersom det inte längre finns tillräckliga skäl för detta. Hon har vidhållit förverkandeyrkandet.

David Ogundedji har begärt frikännande dom och förklarat sig inte ha något att erinra mot förverkandeyrkandet, då narkotikan och emballaget inte är hans.

### SKÄL

Åklagaren har lagt ned åtalet på den grund att det inte finns tillräckliga skäl att David Ogundedji är skyldig till brottet. David Ogundedji har begärt frikännande dom. Hans yrkande ska bifallas.

David Ogundedji har inte haft någon erinran mot förverkandeyrkandet. Det är lagligen grundat och ska bifallas.

### HUR MAN ÖVERKLAGAR, se bilaga (TR-01)

Ett överklagande ställs till Svea hovrätt och ska ha kommit in till tingsrätten senast den 11 januari 2021.

Marianne Carnitz

Bilaga 1

## SVERIGES DOMSTOLAR

**Hur man överklagar**  
Dom i brottmål, tingsrätt

2 av 4

TR-01

Vill du att domen ska ändras i någon del kan du överklaga. Här får du veta hur det går till.

Skicka med skriftliga bevis som inte redan finns i målet.

**Annex 8: Johanna pregnant with her husband David and her daughter-in-law, Daniela at the family company before her husband's detention**

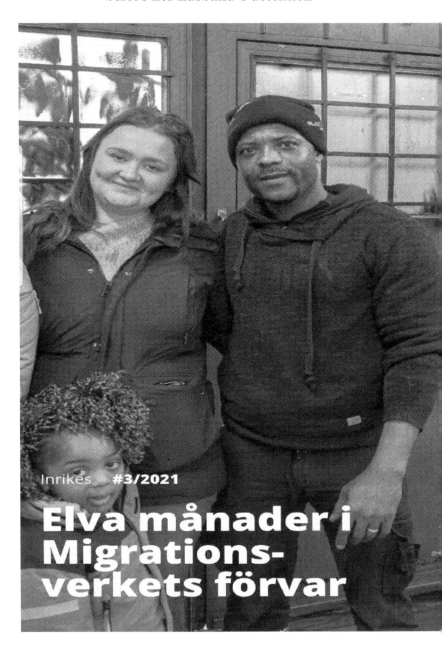

**Annex 9: David saw the first born girl of their marriage from the window of the custody facility since his wife, Johanna was denied visit**

**Annex 10: The father's detention affected the children, Gabriela is crying with a deep sorrow as the picture shows**

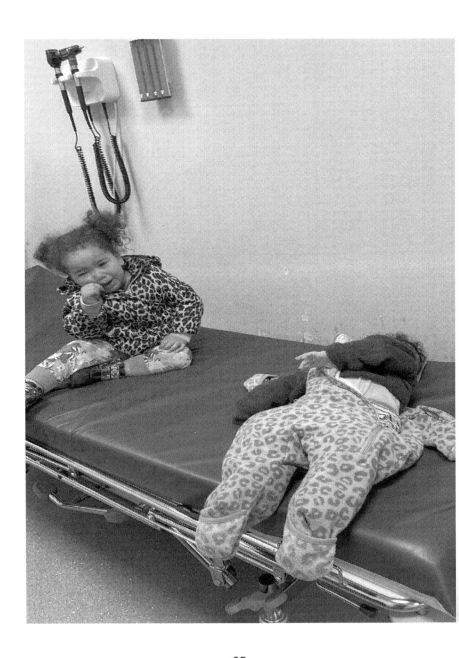

# Annex 11: Attestation of visit the border police

**Polisen**

BESLUT OM UPPSIKT
Enligt utlänningslagen (UtlL)[1]

Sida 2 (3)

Diarienummer
A596.890/2019

☐ på annat sätt hindra verkställigheten av beslutet, därför att

Hur man överklagar

Detta beslut kan överklagas skriftligen till Migrationsdomstolen i Stockholm

Skrivelsen med överklagandet ska emellertid ges in till den polismyndighet som har fattat det överklagande beslutet.
Uppsiktsbeslutet får överklagas när som helst och utan samband med överklagande av avlägsnandebeslutet(14 kap 9 § UBL).

Beslutsfattare, namn och tjänsteställning

**Underskrift m.m.***  ☒ Underskrift av föredraganden på uppdrag av beslutsfattaren

| Datum | Ort | Namnteckning |
|---|---|---|
| 2021-04-05 | Stockholm | |
| Namnförtydligande | | |
| Petra Gardos Ek | | |

* Av beslutsfattaren eller - om beslutet fattas av regeringen eller migrationsverket - den tjänsteman inom polismyndigheten som delger beslutet

**Delgivningsbevis**

| Datum | Ort | Härmed erkännes mottagandet av denna handling |
|---|---|---|
| 5/10-20 | Märsta | Namnteckning |
| Namnförtydligande | | X |
| Kayode David Ogundeji | | |
| Datum | Ort | Beslutet har delgivits av |
| 5/10·20 | Märsta | Namnteckning |
| Namnförtydligande | | Sofie Fagerström |
| Sofie Fagerström | | |

| Foto | Foto | Foto | Foto | Foto |
|---|---|---|---|---|

**Kontaktperson hos Polismyndigheten**

Mattias Halin 010-563 88 68

Ex 1 Behålls av polismyndigheten

96

**Annex 12: The journalist from FARR, Sanna Vestin who took up in a publication released in 2021, the case concerning injustice against David when unlawfully detained in custody for eleven months**

## Annex 13: Family dinner once David back to Sweden (November 2022)